Disney

VILLAINS

Amigurumi

20+ Crochet Patterns for the Unapologetic Crafter

Written by Lee Sartori

SAN RAFAEL • LOS ANGELES • LONDON

Contents

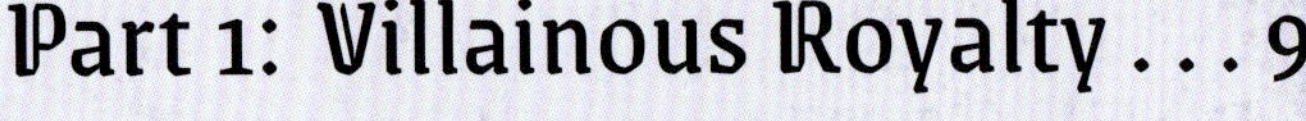

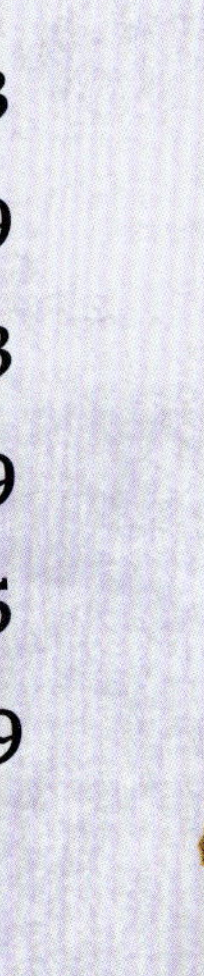

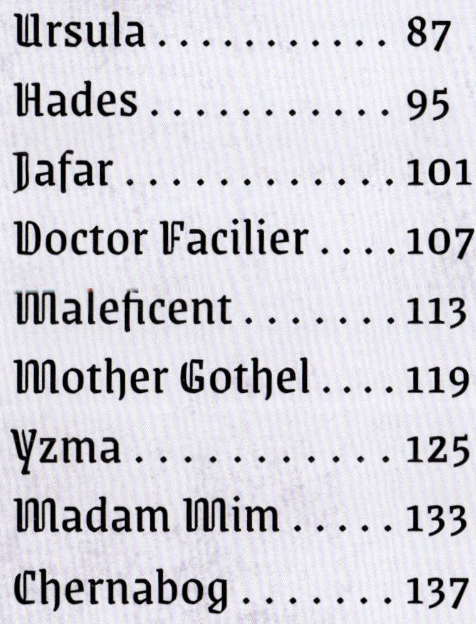

Part 3: Magical Mischief-Makers . . . 85

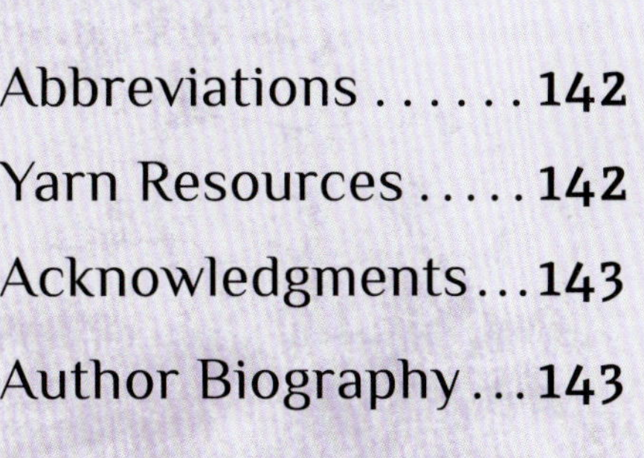

Introduction

In its hundred-plus-year history, Disney has introduced hundreds of heroes to the world. Kindhearted, bright, and brave—their stories bring a bit of magic to everyday life. But what's a hero without a villain? The obstacle to the journey, the thorn on the rose, the mischief in the magic. In this beautiful crochet book, you can experience a bit of the mayhem firsthand, by making your own amigurumi versions of iconic Disney Villains. Each of the twenty-one villains in this book *could* be called evil. In fact, many of them have been! They *are* mischievous troublemakers with their own agendas. And they *do* behave badly. But they are also passionate and determined, and some may say *they're* the heroes of their own story. Disney Villains come in all stripes: some were born royal, or with a flair for magic, while others were just born to plan and plot. Ultimately, these schemers and misbehavers have managed to endear themselves to fans, to make a lasting impact across generations and even eras. Plus, they're a lot less frightening in crochet form!

Within the pages of this book, you'll find patterns for crocheting villains from the 1940s to the 2000s (and beyond). The finished pieces could be called "dolls" or "stuffed yarn plushies" depending on who you ask. They also largely fall into the category known as *amigurumi*, a Japanese term for "crocheting in the round." It's a word typically reserved for crocheted characters that are mainly shaped from circles.

From *Sleeping Beauty*'s spurned Maleficent to *Moana*'s Tamatoa, these villains appear extra cute in crochet form. It can be easy to forget their devious intentions, so don't drop your guard (or forget to track your progress with a stitch marker)! Then again, without Ursula, would Ariel have truly become part of that world? Without Hades, would Hercules have found his "hero" status? So, enjoy this little bit of mischief and, of course, embrace crocheting in your villain era!

To my big brother, Dustin, who watched our VHS copy of *The Lion King* on repeat with me so that we could learn all the words to every song. I love you!

Part 1

Villainous Royalty

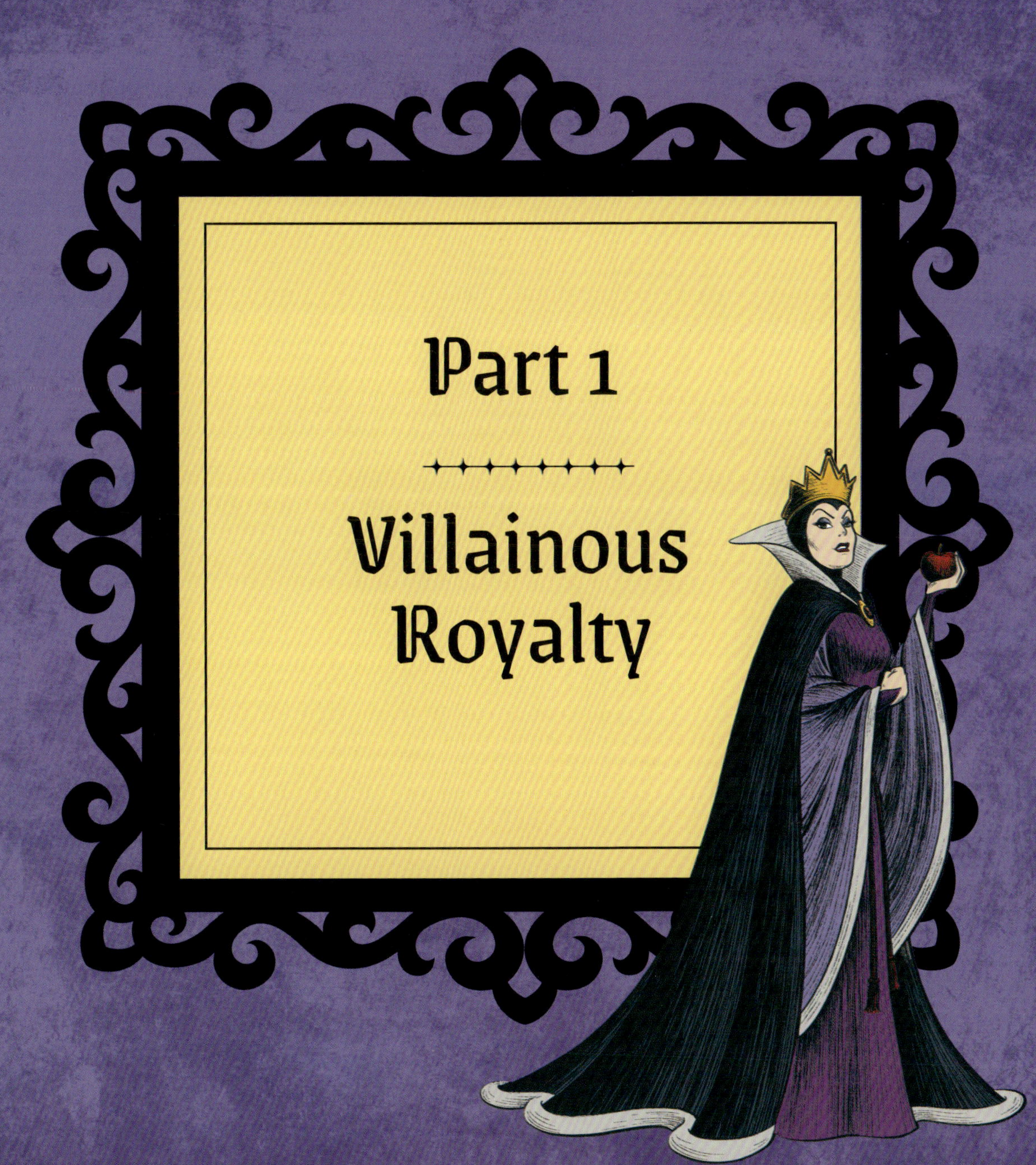

The Evil Queen

Designed by Lee Sartori

Skill Level: Intermediate

The kingdom's beautiful Evil Queen has style, grace, and magical powers. She also has a certain stepdaughter who seems to be beloved by all, and a Magic Mirror willing to attest to that.

There are countless warnings to be had about vanity, and the Evil Queen may be a perfect representation of what can go wrong when that advice is ignored. When her Magic Mirror's answers stir up her jealousy of Snow White, the Evil Queen lashes out. Snow White flees to the forest and takes refuge with seven dwarfs who become her dear friends. Never one to settle, the Evil Queen seeks to remove her competition entirely, with a poison apple. To enact her plan, she drinks a potion disguising her as a peddler, giving up her typically stately appearance for a time. Some might point out the irony in that . . .

Fairest or not, we think this crocheted version of the Evil Queen from *Snow White and the Seven Dwarfs* is pretty cute! Her long purple gown and her shiny golden crown add to her powerful appearance. And if any apples look especially enticing while you work on this project . . . maybe keep her in another room during your next snack break.

"Don't let the wish grow cold!"

—The Evil Queen, *Snow White and the Seven Dwarfs* (1937)

YARN

Worsted weight (#4 medium) yarn, shown in Lion Brand Basic Stitch Anti Pilling™ (100% acrylic, 185 yd. / 170 m per 3.5 oz. / 100 g skein)

Color A: #121L Almond, 1 skein
Color B: #147B Purple, 1 skein
Color C: #153 Black, 1 skein
Color D: #158L Mustard, 1 skein
Color E: #400G Red Heather, 1 skein
Color F: #112S Deco Rose, 1 skein
Color G: #100 White, 1 skein

HOOK

US D (3.25 mm) crochet hook

NOTIONS

Pair of 12 mm black safety eyes
Stitch markers
Polyester stuffing
Yarn needle
Scissors

FINISHED MEASUREMENTS

Height: 14" / 35.5 cm
Width: 7" / 17.75 cm

SPECIAL STITCHES

Inc (increase) = Work 2 sc in the next st.

Invdec (invisible single crochet decrease) = Insert hook in front loop only of each of next 2 sts, yo and draw through both sts, yo and draw through 2 loops on hook—1 st decreased.

Popcorn (popcorn stitch) = Work 5 dc in next st, drop loop on hook, insert hook from front to back in first dc made, place dropped loop on hook and draw through dc.

Sc2tog (single crochet 2 together) = [Insert hook in next st, yo and draw up a loop] twice, yo and draw through all loops on hook—1 st decreased.

Picot = Ch 3, sl st in 3rd ch from hook.

GAUGE

28 sc and 28 rnds = 4 in. / 10 cm in sc

Gauge is not critical for this project. Ensure your stitches are tight so the stuffing won't show through.

NOTES

- Work in continuous rounds unless otherwise indicated.
- When indicated, join at the end of a round with a slip stitch in the first stitch. To join new yarn to a stitch, insert hook in stitch and pull up a loop in indicated color.
- To change colors, work the last yarn over of the previous stitch with the new color. Fasten off previous color unless otherwise indicated.
- If desired, instead of making a magic ring, chain 2 and work indicated stitches in the 2nd chain from the hook.

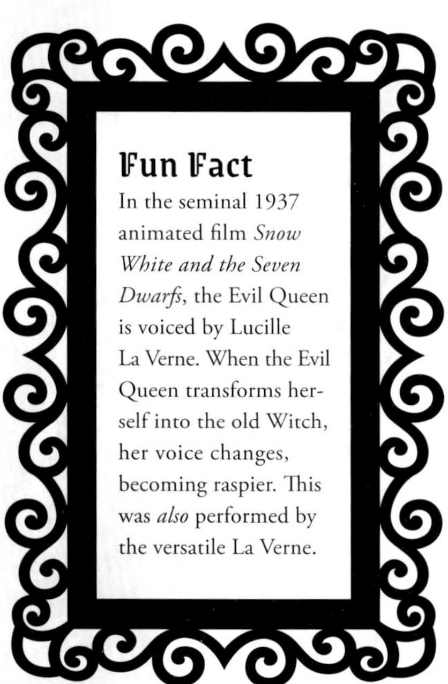

Fun Fact

In the seminal 1937 animated film *Snow White and the Seven Dwarfs*, the Evil Queen is voiced by Lucille La Verne. When the Evil Queen transforms herself into the old Witch, her voice changes, becoming raspier. This was *also* performed by the versatile La Verne.

Arms (Make 2)

With **A** make a magic ring.
Rnd 1: 6 sc in ring—6 sc.
Rnd 2: Inc around—12 sc.
Rnds 3–4: Sc around.
Rnd 5: Popcorn, sc 11.
Rnds 6–7: Sc around.
Rnd 8: [Invdec, sc 2] around, join—9 sc.
Change to **B**.
Rnd 9: Ch 1, working in BLO sc around, join.
Rnd 10: Ch 1 tightly, [sc, inc, sc] around, join—12 sc.
Rnds 11–24: Sc around.
Fasten off. Weave in ends. Stuff Arm lightly. Set aside to join to Body.

Body

With **B** make a magic ring.
Rnd 1: 6 sc in ring—6 sc.
Rnd 2: Inc around—12 sc.
Rnd 3: [Inc, sc] around—18 sc.
Rnd 4: [Sc, inc, sc] around—24 sc.
Rnd 5: [Inc, sc 3] around—30 sc.
Rnd 6: [Sc 2, inc, sc 2] around—36 sc.
Rnd 7: [Inc, sc 5] around—42 sc.
Rnd 8: [Sc 3, inc, sc 3] around—48 sc.
Rnd 9: [Inc, sc 7] around—54 sc.
Rnd 10: Working in BLO, [sc 4, inc, sc 4] around—60 sc.
Rnd 11: [Inc, sc 9] around—66 sc.
Rnd 12: [Sc 5, inc, sc 5] around, join—72 sc.
Rnd 13: Ch 1, working in BLO, sc in first st and mark unworked FL with st marker, sc around, join.
Rnd 14: Ch 1 tightly, [sc 5, invdec, sc 5] around, do not join—66 sc.
Rnd 15: [Sc 10, invdec, sc 10] around—63 sc.
Rnd 16: [Invdec, sc 19] around—60 sc.
Rnd 17: [Sc 9, invdec, sc 9] around—57 sc.
Rnd 18: [Invdec, sc 17] around—54 sc.
Rnd 19: [Sc 8, invdec, sc 8] around—51 sc.
Rnd 20: [Invdec, sc 15] around—48 sc.
Rnd 21: [Sc 7, invdec, sc 7] around—45 sc.
Rnd 22: [Invdec, sc 13] around—42 sc.
Rnd 23: [Sc 6, invdec, sc 6] around—39 sc.
Rnd 24: [Invdec, sc 11] around—36 sc.
Rnds 25–44: Sc around.
Stuff and continue stuffing as work progresses.
Hold Arms in line with Body to join in next rnd.
Rnd 45: Sc 9 on Body, sc 12 around first Arm to join, sc 18 on Body, sc 12 around 2nd Arm to join, sc 9 on Body—60 sc.
Rnds 46–50: Sc around.
Rnd 51: [Sc 4, invdec, sc 4] around—54 sc.
Rnd 52: [Invdec, sc 7] around—48 sc.
Rnd 53: [Sc 3, invdec, sc 3] around—42 sc.
Rnd 54: [Invdec, sc 5] around—36 sc.
Rnd 55: [Sc 2, invdec, sc 2] around—30 sc.
Change to **C**.
Rnd 56: [Invdec, sc 3] around—24 sc.

Rnd 57: [Sc, invdec, sc] around—18 sc.
Stuff Body and tops of Arms.
Continue to Head.

Head

Continuing with **C**.
Rnd 1: Sc around—18 sc.
Rnd 2: Ch 1, sc around, join.
Rnd 3: Ch 1 tightly, inc around, do not join—36 sc.
Rnd 4: [Inc, sc 5] around—42 sc.
Rnd 5: [Sc 3, inc, sc 3] around, join—48 sc.
Change to **A**.
Rnd 6: Ch 1, working in BLO [inc, sc 7] around, join—54 sc.
Rnd 7: Ch 1 tightly, sc around, do not join.
Rnds 8–20: Sc around.
Add safety eyes between Rnds 15 and 16 approximately 8 sts apart. Using a length of **C**, embroider eyebrows above eyes using photos as a guide. Using a length of **A** held double, embroider nose between Rnds 13 and 14 over 3 sts.
Rnd 21: [Invdec, sc 7] around—48 sc.
Rnd 22: [Sc 3, invdec, sc 3] around—42 sc.
Rnd 23: [Invdec, sc 5] around—36 sc.
Rnd 24: [Sc 2, invdec, sc 2] around—30 sc.
Stuff Head and continue stuffing as work progresses.
Rnd 25: [Invdec, sc 3] around—24 sc.
Rnd 26: [Sc, invdec, sc] around—18 sc.
Rnd 27: [Invdec, sc] around—12 sc.
Rnd 28: Invdec around—6 sc.

Fasten off, leaving a long tail for sewing. Sew remaining 6 sts closed. Weave in end.

Head Piece

With **C** make a magic ring.
Rnd 1: 6 sc in ring—6 sc.
Rnd 2: Inc around—12 sc.
Rnd 3: [Inc, sc] around—18 sc.
Rnd 4: [Sc, inc, sc] around—24 sc.
Rnd 5: [Inc, sc 3] around—30 sc.
Rnd 6: [Sc 2, inc, sc 2] around—36 sc.
Rnd 7: [Inc, sc 5] around—42 sc.
Rnd 8: [Sc 3, inc, sc 3] around—48 sc.
Rnd 9: [Inc, sc 7] around—54 sc.
Rnds 10–14: Sc around.
Begin working in turned rows.
Row 15: Sc 8, turn, leaving remaining sts unworked—8 sc.
Row 16: Ch 1, sc2tog, sc 4, sc2tog, turn—6 sc.
Row 17: Ch 1, sc2tog, sc 2, sc2tog, turn—4 sc.
Row 18: Ch 1, [sc2tog] twice, turn—2 sc.
Row 19: Ch 1, sc2tog, do not turn—1 sc.
Rnd 20: Ch 1, sc 5 across row ends, sc 46 around unworked sts of Rnd 14, sc 5 across row ends, sc in sc of Row 19, join—57 sc.

Fasten off, leaving a long tail for sewing. Sew Head Piece to top of Head, with Row 19 resting between eyes and with the back touching the last round made with **C**. Weave in ends.

Head Piece Sides (Make 2)

This piece is made to fill the gap between the Head Piece and the neck.
With **C**.
Row 1: Ch 2, sc in 2nd ch from hook, turn—1 sc.
Row 2: Ch 1, inc, turn—2 sc.
Row 3: Ch 1, inc, sc, turn—3 sc.
Row 4: Ch 1, sc 2, inc, turn—4 sc.
Row 5: Ch 1, inc, sc 3, turn—5 sc.
Row 6: Ch 1, sc 4, inc—6 sc.
Fasten off, leaving a long tail for sewing. Sew to sides of face in gap between neck and Head Piece. Weave in ends.

Crown

With **D** leave a long tail at start for sewing.
Rnd 1: Ch 48, sl st to 1st ch to form a ring, ch 1, sc in each ch around, join—48 sc.
Rnd 2: Ch 1, sc around, join.
Begin working in turned rows.
Row 3 (first 2 triangles): Ch 1, sc 12, [sc, ch 6, starting in 2nd ch from hook sc, hdc, dc, tr 2, continuing on Rnd 2, skip next 2 sts, sc] twice, sc

8, mark next st with st marker, turn leaving marked st and remaining sts unworked—34 sts.

Row 4 (center triangle): Ch 1, sc2tog, sc 6, turn—7 sc.

Row 5: Ch 1, sc2tog, sc 5, turn—6 sc.

Row 6: Ch 1, sc2tog, sc 4, turn—5 sc.

Row 7: Ch 1, sc2tog, sc 3, turn—4 sc.

Row 8: Ch 1, sc2tog, sc 2, turn—3 sc.

Row 9: Ch 1, sc2tog, sc, turn—2 sc.

Row 10: Ch 1, sc2tog, turn—1 sc.

Row 11: Ch 1, sc.

Fasten off. Join in marked st of Row 3 (the next unworked st after the base of the center triangle).

Rnd 12: Ch 1, [sc, ch 6, starting in 2nd ch from hook sc, hdc, dc, tr 2, continuing on unworked sts of Rnd 2, skip next 2 sts, sc] twice, sc in remaining unworked sts of Rnd 2, join—26 sts.

Rnd 13: Ch 1, sc 13, *sc in underside of next 5 chs, (sc, picot, sc) in skipped ch, sc in next 5 sts of triangle*, sc in next 2 sc, repeat from * to * once, sc in next sc, sc 8 evenly up row ends of center triangle, (sc, picot, sc) in sc at top of triangle, sc 8 evenly down opposite row ends, sc in next sc, repeat from * to * once, sc in next 2 sc, repeat from * to * once, sc 13, join—98 sc.

Fasten off. Using starting tail, sew Crown to top of Head. Weave in ends.

Belt

With **E** ch 100.

Fasten off and tie around waist of Body.

Sleeves (Make 2)

With **F**.

Row 1: Ch 4, starting in 2nd ch from hook sc across, turn—3 sc.

Row 2: Ch 1, sc 2, inc, turn—4 sc.

Row 3: Ch 1, inc, sc 3, turn—5 sc.

Row 4: Ch 1, sc 4, inc, turn—6 sc.

Row 5: Ch 1, inc, sc 5, turn—7 sc.

Row 6: Ch 1, sc 6, inc, turn—8 sc.

Row 7: Ch 1, inc, sc 7, turn—9 sc.

Row 8: Ch 1, sc 8, inc, turn—10 sc.

Row 9: Ch 1, inc, sc 9, turn—11 sc.

Row 10: Ch 1, sc 10, inc, turn—12 sc.

Rows 11–60: Ch 1, sc across, turn.

Row 61: Ch 1, sc2tog, sc 10, turn—11 sc.

Row 62: Ch 1, sc 9, sc2tog, turn—10 sc.

Row 63: Ch 1, sc2tog, sc 8, turn—9 sc.

Row 64: Ch 1, sc 7, sc2tog, turn—8 sc.

Row 65: Ch 1, sc2tog, sc 6, turn—7 sc.

Row 66: Ch 1, sc 5, sc2tog, turn—6 sc.

Row 67: Ch 1, sc2tog, sc 4, turn—5 sc.

Row 68: Ch 1, sc 3, sc2tog, turn—4 sc.

Row 69: Ch 1, sc2tog, sc 2, do not turn—3 sc.

Rnd 70 (border): Ch 1, working in row ends of straight edge, sc 68 evenly across, inc in underside of starting ch (mark first of these 2 sts with a st marker), inc in each of the next 2 chs, sc 68 evenly across opposite side row ends, inc in next 3 sts of Row 69 (mark the last st with a st marker)—148 sc.

Fasten off and continue to Sleeve Ribbing.

Sleeve Ribbing

With **G**, repeat instructions for each Sleeve.

Join to first marked st of Sleeve.

Row 1: Ch 4, sc in 2nd ch from hook and in next 2 chs, working in BLO, sl st in next 2 sts of Rnd 70 of Sleeve—3 sc.

Row 2: Ch 1, turn, skip 2 sl sts, working in BLO, sc in next 3 sc—3 sc.

Row 3: Ch 1, turn, working in BLO throughout, sc 3, sl st in next 2 sts of Rnd 70 of Sleeve—3 sc.

Rows 4–73: Repeat Rows 2–3 across to next marked st of Sleeve. Fasten off. Drape Sleeve over Arm. Using a length of **F**, seam the bottom 3" of the inside edge of the Sleeve closed. Using **F** secure Sleeve to Arm. Weave in ends.

"All alone, my pet?"

—The Evil Queen, *Snow White and the Seven Dwarfs* (1937)

Collar

With **G** leave a long tail at start for sewing.

Row 1: Ch 19, starting in 2nd ch from hook, sc across, turn—18 sc.

Row 2: Ch 1, [sc, inc, sc] across, turn—24 sc.

Row 3: Ch 1, [inc, sc 3] across, turn—30 sc.

Row 4: Ch 1, [sc 2, inc, sc 2] across, turn—36 sc.

Row 5: Ch 1, [inc, sc 5] across, turn—42 sc.

Row 6: Ch 1, [sc 3, inc, sc 3] across, turn—48 sc.

Row 7: Ch 1, [inc, sc 7] across—54 sc.

Fasten off. Weave in end. Using starting tail, sew around base of neck.

Jewel

With **E** make a magic ring.

Rnd 1: 6 sc in ring, join—6 sc.

Change to **D**.

Rnd 2: Ch 1, sl st in each st around, join.

Fasten off and sew to front of chest, adding a length of **G** to act as a necklace.

Cape

With **C** leave a long tail at the start for sewing.

Row 1: Ch 27, starting in 4th ch from hook (skipped chs count as first dc) dc across, turn—25 dc.

Row 2: Ch 3 (*counts as a st*), dc in same st (*increase made*), dc across, turn—26 dc.

Rows 3–21: Repeat Row 2—45 dc at end of Row 21.

Rnd 22 (border): Ch 1, sc across, ch 1, rotate to work 38 sc evenly across row ends, ch 1, sc 25 in underside of chs, ch 1, sc 38 evenly across opposite edge row ends, ch 1, join—146 sc.

Fasten off, weave in end. Using starting tail, sew to back of neck. Weave in end.

Skirt

With **B** join in marked FL of Rnd 13 of Body.

Rnd 1: Ch 2 (*does not count as a st here and throughout*), dc in unworked FLO around, join—72 dc.

Rnd 2: Ch 2, [2 dc in next st, dc 11] around, join—78 dc.

Rnd 3: Ch 2, [dc 6, 2 dc in next st, dc 6] around, join—84 dc.

Rnd 4: Ch 2, [2 dc in next st, dc 13] around, join—90 dc.

Rnd 5: Ch 2, [dc 7, 2 dc in next st, dc 7] around, join—96 dc.

Fasten off. Weave in ends.

Scar

Designed by Lee Sartori

Skill Level: Intermediate

The savanna is abuzz with news of the arrival of King Mufasa's new cub, Simba. However, Mufasa's younger brother, Scar, is not amused. It was less than ideal when Scar was second in line to the royal throne in this lion pride. Being pushed even further from the crown by an infant is just . . . no reason to jump for joy. Mufasa's reign is shaping up to be a long one with a lasting legacy. And that just won't do. Besides, all of Scar's hyena friends say he is the best lion for the job! Scar has meticulous plans for the kingdom and they don't include his brother Mufasa, or his annoying little progeny. Mufasa and Simba better watch their backs and be prepared.

We've got sensational news of our own! We've prepared the most adorable version of Scar for you to crochet. His claws are out, his mane is shaggy, and his sneer is oh-so-evil. Using easy crochet stitches and fun construction, your little version of Scar can't get into too much trouble . . . at least we hope not.

"You know the law. Never, ever mention that name in my presence. I am the king!"

—Scar, *The Lion King* (1994)

YARN

Worsted weight (#4 medium) yarn, shown in Lion Brand Basic Stitch Anti Pilling™ (100% acrylic, 185 yd. / 170 m per 3.5 oz. / 100 g skein)

Color A: #122T Hazelnut, 1 skein

Color B: #134U Honey, 2 skeins

Color C: #153 Black, 1 skein

HOOK

US D (3.25 mm) crochet hook

NOTIONS

Yellow felt
Black felt
Lime green felt
Dark pink embroidery thread
Hole punch
Thin-tipped permanent marker
Glue
Stitch marker
Polyester stuffing
Yarn needle
Scissors

FINISHED MEASUREMENTS

Height: 9" / 22.5 cm
Width: 7" / 17.5 cm

SPECIAL STITCHES

Inc (increase) = Work 2 sc in the next st.

Invdec (invisible single crochet decrease) = Insert hook in front loop only of each of next 2 sts, yo and draw through both sts, yo and draw through 2 loops on hook—1 st decreased.

GAUGE

28 sc and 28 rnds = 4 in. / 10 cm in sc

Gauge is not critical for this project. Ensure your stitches are tight so the stuffing won't show through.

NOTES

- Work in continuous rounds unless otherwise indicated.
- When indicated, join at the end of a round with a slip stitch in the first stitch. To join new yarn to a stitch, insert hook in stitch and pull up a loop in indicated color.
- To change colors, work the last yarn over of the previous stitch with the new color. Fasten off previous color unless otherwise indicated.
- If desired, instead of making a magic ring, chain 2 and work indicated stitches in the 2nd chain from the hook.

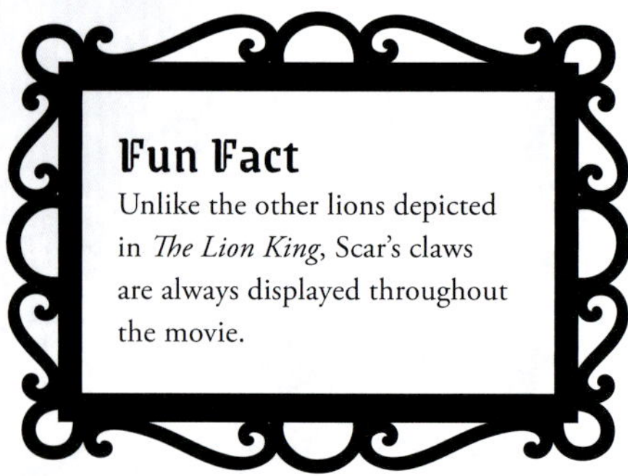

Fun Fact
Unlike the other lions depicted in *The Lion King*, Scar's claws are always displayed throughout the movie.

"Oh, and just between us, you might want to work on that little roar of yours."

—Scar, *The Lion King* (1994)

Single Toes (Make 12)

With **A** make a magic ring.
Rnd 1: 6 sc in ring—6 sc.
Rnd 2: Sc around.
Fasten off.

Feet (Make 4)

Make a Single Toe, but do not fasten off.
Next rnd will join current Toe with 3 additional Single Toes together.
Rnd 1: Sc 3 on current Toe, sc 3 on each of next 2 Toes, sc 6 around last Toe, sc 3 on backside of each of 2 center Toes, sc 3 on current Toe—24 sc.
Rnd 2: Sc around.
Change to **B**.
Rnd 3: Ch 1, working in BLO, sc around, join—24 sc.
Rnd 4: Ch 1, [sc 3, invdec, sc 3] around, join—21 sc.
Rnds 5–7: Sc around.
Rnd 8: Ch 1, sc 2, ch 7, skip next 7 sts (*leg opening made*), sc 12, join—14 sc, 7 chs.
Rnd 9: Ch 1, sc in each ch and st around, join—21 sc.
Rnd 10: Ch 1, [invdec, sc 5] around, join—18 sc.
Rnd 11: Ch 1, [invdec, sc] around, join—12 sc.
Rnd 12: Ch 1, invdec around, join—6 sc.
Fasten off, leaving a long tail for sewing. Sew remaining 6 sts closed. Weave in end. Stuff Foot.

Back Legs (Make 2)

With **B** join to first skipped sc of Rnd 7 of Foot.
Rnd 1: Ch 1, sc 7 in skipped sc, sc in gap before underside of ch-7, sc in underside of next 7 chs, sc in gap before first sc, join—16 sc.
Rnd 2: Ch 1 tightly, [inc, sc 7] around, do not join—18 sc.
Rnds 3–7: Sc around.
Rnd 8: [Sc, inc, sc] around—24 sc.
Rnd 9: Sc around.
Rnd 10: [Sc, invdec, sc] around—18 sc.
Rnd 11: [Invdec, sc] around—12 sc.
Stuff.
Rnd 12: Invdec around—6 sc.
Fasten off, leaving a long tail for sewing. Sew remaining 6 sts closed.

Front Legs (Make 2)

With **B** join to first skipped sc of Rnd 7 of Foot.

Rnd 1: Ch 1, sc 7 in skipped sc, sc in gap before underside of ch-7, sc in underside of next 7 chs, sc in gap before first sc, join—16 sc.

Rnds 2–12: Sc around.

Fasten off. Stuff Leg. Set aside to join to Body.

Body

With **B** make a magic ring.

Rnd 1: 6 sc in ring—6 sc.

Rnd 2: Inc around—12 sc.

Rnd 3: [Inc, sc] around—18 sc.

Rnd 4: [Sc, inc, sc] around—24 sc.

Rnd 5: [Inc, sc 3] around—30 sc.

Rnd 6: [Sc 2, inc, sc 2] around—36 sc.

Rnd 7: [Inc, sc 5] around—42 sc.

Rnd 8: [Sc 3, inc, sc 3] around—48 sc.

Rnd 9: [Inc, sc 7] around—54 sc.

Rnds 10–24: Sc around.

Rnd 25: [Invdec, sc 7] around—48 sc.

Hold Front Legs in line with Body to join in next rnd.

Rnd 26: Sc 3, sc in center back st of 1st Front Leg, sc 15 around 1st Front Leg, sc 9 on Body, sc in center back st of 2nd Front Leg, sc 15 around 2nd Front Leg, sc 36 on Body—80 sc.

Rnd 27: Sc around.

Rnd 28: [Sc 4, invdec, sc 4] around—72 sc.

Rnd 29: Sc around.

Rnd 30: [Sc 5, invdec, sc 5] around—66 sc.

Rnd 31: Sc around.

Rnd 32: [Invdec, sc 9] around—60 sc.

Rnd 33: Sc around.

Rnd 34: [Sc 4, invdec, sc 4] around—54 sc.

Rnd 35: Sc around.

Rnd 36: [Invdec, sc 7] around—48 sc.

Rnds 37–39: Sc around.

Rnd 40: [Sc 3, invdec, sc 3] around—42 sc.

Rnd 41: Sc around.

Rnd 42: [Invdec, sc 5] around—36 sc.

Rnd 43: Sc around.

Rnd 44: [Sc 2, invdec, sc 2] around—30 sc.

Rnd 45: Sc around.

Sew Back Legs to either side of Body. Continue to Head.

Head

With **B**.

Rnd 1: Inc around—60 sc.

Rnds 2–9: Sc around.

Rnd 10: [Sc 9, invdec, sc 9] around—57 sc.

Rnd 11: [Invdec, sc 17] around—54 sc.

Rnd 12: [Sc 8, invdec, sc 8] around—51 sc.

Rnd 13: [Invdec, sc 15] around—48 sc.

Rnd 14: [Sc 3, invdec, sc 3] around—42 sc.

Rnd 15: [Invdec, sc 5] around—36 sc.

Rnd 16: [Sc 2, invdec, sc 2] around—30 sc.

Stuff Head. Continue stuffing as work progresses.

Rnd 17: [Invdec, sc 3] around—24 sc.

Rnd 18: [Sc, invdec, sc] around—18 sc.

Rnd 19: [Invdec, sc] around—12 sc.

Rnd 20: Invdec around—6 sc.

Fasten off, leaving a long tail for sewing. Sew remaining 6 sts closed. Weave in end.

Lower Jaw

With **A**.

Rnd 1: Ch 5, starting in 2nd ch from hook, sc 3, 3 sc in last ch, rotate to work in underside of ch, sc 3, 3 sc in skipped ch—12 sc.

Rnd 2: *Sc 3, inc 3; repeat from * around—18 sc.

Rnd 3: *Sc 3, [inc, sc] 3 times; repeat from * around—24 sc.

Rnds 4–6: Sc around.

Fasten off, leaving a long tail for sewing. Stuff piece. Sew Lower Jaw to Head between Rnds 1 and 5 of Head. Weave in ends.

Muzzle

With **A** make a magic ring.

Rnd 1: 6 sc in ring—6 sc.

Rnd 2: Inc around—12 sc.

Rnd 3: [Inc, sc] around—18 sc.

Rnd 4: Sc around.

Begin working in rows.

Row 5: Sc 6, hdc 3, [2 dc in next st] 6 times, hdc 3, turn—24 sts.

Row 6: Ch 1, hdc 3, dc 12, hdc 3, leave remaining sts unworked—18 sts.

Fasten off, leaving a long tail for sewing. Stuff piece. Sew Muzzle directly above Lower Jaw, between Rnds 5 and 10 of Head.

Nose

With **B**.

Row 1: Ch 5, starting in 2nd ch from hook, sc across, turn—4 sc.

Row 2: Ch 1, inc, sc 2, inc, turn—6 sc.

Rows 3–6: Ch 1, sc across, turn.

Fasten off, leaving a long tail for sewing. Sew Nose on top of Muzzle, with the last row of the Nose touching Rnd 10 of Head.

Nose Tip

With **C**.

Row 1: Ch 2, 3 sc in 2nd ch from hook, turn—3 sc.

Row 2: (Ch 2, dc, ch 2) in first st, (sc, ch 2) in next st, 2 dc in last st—4 sts.

Fasten off, leaving a long tail for sewing. Sew Nose Tip to bottom of Nose. Weave in ends.

Inner Ears (Make 2)

With **C** make a magic ring.

Rnd 1: 6 sc in ring—6 sc.

Rnd 2: Inc around—12 sc.

Fasten off, leaving a long tail for sewing.

Outer Ears (Make 2)

With **B** make a magic ring.

Rnd 1: 6 sc in ring—6 sc.

Rnd 2: Inc around—12 sc.

Rnd 3 (joining): Holding an Inner Ear and an Outer Ear together and stitching through both thicknesses to join, [inc, sc] around, join—18 sc.

Rnd 4: Ch 1, sc around.

Fasten off, leaving a long tail for sewing. Sew to sides of Head in line with eyeline. Weave in ends.

Eyebrows (Make 2)

With **B**.

Row 1: Ch 12.

Fasten off, leaving a long tail for sewing.

Top Hair Piece

With **C**.

Row 1: Ch 17, starting in 2nd ch from hook, sc across, turn—16 sc.

Row 2: Ch 1, working in BLO, sc across.

Fasten off, leaving a long tail for sewing. Sew lengthwise from top of Head down back of neck.

Chest Hair Piece

With **C**.

Row 1: Ch 31, starting in 2nd ch from hook, sc across, turn—30 sc.

Row 2: Ch 1, working in BLO, sc across.

Fasten off, leaving a long tail for sewing. Sew under chin and around face. Weave in ends.

Belly Patch

With **A**.

Row 1: Ch 7, starting in 2nd ch from hook, sc across, turn—6 sc.

Rows 2–27: Ch 1, sc across, turn.

Rnd 28: Ch 1, sc in each st and row end around entire piece, join—66 sc.

Tail

With **B** make a magic ring. Stuff shape very lightly as work progresses.

Rnd 1: 6 sc in ring—6 sc.

Rnds 2–32: Sc around.

Fasten off, leaving a long tail for sewing. Sew Tail to bottom back of Body. Using several lengths of **C**, add fringe to bottom of Tail.

Finishing

To make eyes, use a standard hole punch to punch out 2 circles of lime green felt for the inner eye. Use a thin-tipped permanent marker to mark a pupil in each eye. Using photos as a guide, cut yellow shape from yellow felt and glue to inner eye. Using black felt, cut out final eye shape for socket and glue yellow layer to black socket. Glue finished eye to each side of face, touching the top edge of the Nose. Sew an Eyebrow above each eye.

Using **A**, cut approximately 10 pieces of yarn 3" long, and to bottom of Lower Jaw using lark's head knot. Trim using photos as a guide.

Using **C**, cut approximately 60 pieces of hair measuring 6" long and, holding 2 strands together, attach to the sides of the Top Hair Piece using lark's head knot. Add any extra strands to the very front to fill hairline in fully. Some hair should fall in front of the ears while the rest will fall down the back of the neck.

Using **C**, cut approximately 60 pieces of hair measuring 6" long and, holding 2 strands together, attach to Chest Hair Piece using lark's head knot. Trim using photos as a guide.

Using **C**, add straight stitches for small claws to the front of each of the Toes.

Using pink embroidery thread, add a scar above and below left eye.

Prince John

Designed by Sarah Csiacsek

Skill Level: Intermediate

There's something afoot in Sherwood Forest. More specifically, the rogue known as Robin Hood has been stealing from the wealthy . . . and giving his loot to the poor, overtaxed villagers of Nottingham. This is decidedly not what Prince John hoped for when he usurped the throne from his brother, King Richard, who happens to be away in battle at the moment. The kingdom's riches and treasures are supposed to be Prince John's to enjoy. And if that means raising taxes on his citizens, well then, so be it! It is hard enough for Prince John to enjoy the wealth and comfort of his new position without his dear mother around to see how well he has done for himself. But no matter. He'll sleep in the comfort of his kingly bed with his cuddly bag of money to soothe him. It would take an awfully cunning plan from Robin Hood to rob Prince John of the trappings of his newfound kingly life . . .

You can call him "Prince" or you can call him "King," but either way Prince John is dressed to impress! With his glittery crown and his royal red coat, he is ready to rule the kingdom with an iron fist. We think that this crocheted version of Prince John would be much nicer to cuddle than a bag of money, don't you?

"Enough! I am king! King! King!"

—Prince John, *Robin Hood* (1973)

YARN

Worsted weight (#4 medium) yarn, shown in WeCrochet Swish (100% fine superwash merino wool, 110 yd. / 100 m per 1.75 oz. / 50 g ball)

Color A: Black, 1 ball
Color B: White, 1 ball
Color C: Allspice, 1 ball
Color D: Serene, 1 ball
Color E: Dijon, 1 ball
Color F: Phoenix, 1 ball
Color G: Clementine, 1 ball

HOOK

US G (4 mm) crochet hook

NOTIONS

Pair of 9 mm black safety eyes
5 mm red and green acrylic rhinestones
3 mm red acrylic rhinestones
Glue
14 gauge aluminum wire
Stitch markers
Polyester stuffing
Yarn needle
Scissors

FINISHED MEASUREMENTS

Height: 8" / 20 cm
Width: 3"/ 7.5 cm

GAUGE

20 sts and 24 rnds = 4 in. / 10 cm in sc

Gauge is not critical for this project. Ensure your stitches are tight so the stuffing won't show through.

SPECIAL STITCHES

Inc (increase) = Work 2 sc in the next st.

Invdec (invisible single crochet decrease) = Insert hook in front loop only of each of next 2 sts, yo and draw through both sts, yo and draw through 2 loops on hook—1 st decreased.

Bobble (bobble stitch) = [Yo, insert hook into st, yo and draw up a loop, yo and draw through 2 loops on hook] 5 times, yo and draw through all loops on hook.

Picot = Ch 3, inserting hook in FL and the vertical bar of last st made made, sl st.

NOTES

- Work in continuous rounds unless otherwise indicated.
- When indicated, join at the end of a round with a slip stitch in the first stitch. To join new yarn to a stitch, insert hook in stitch and pull up a loop in indicated color.
- To change colors, work the last yarn over of the previous stitch with the new color. Fasten off previous color unless otherwise indicated.
- If desired, instead of making a magic ring, chain 2 and work indicated stitches in the 2nd chain from the hook.

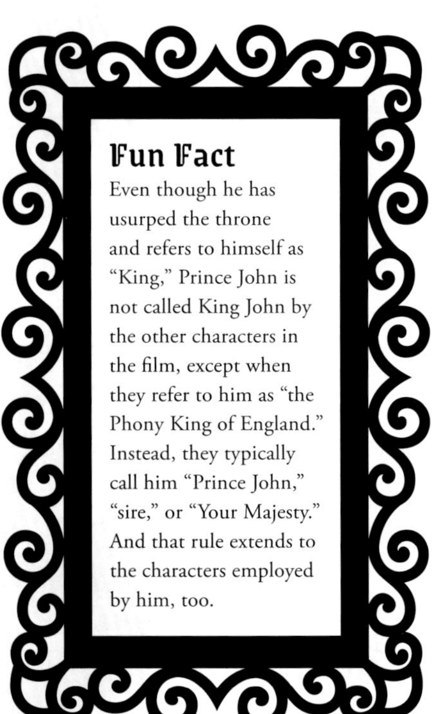

Fun Fact

Even though he has usurped the throne and refers to himself as "King," Prince John is not called King John by the other characters in the film, except when they refer to him as "the Phony King of England." Instead, they typically call him "Prince John," "sire," or "Your Majesty." And that rule extends to the characters employed by him, too.

Legs (Make 2)

With **C**.

Rnd 1: Ch 5, starting in 2nd ch from hook, sc 3, 3 sc in last ch, rotate to work in underside of starting ch, sc 2, inc, join—10 sc.

Rnd 2: Ch 1, inc, sc 2, inc 3, sc 2, inc 2, join—16 sc.

Rnd 3: Ch 1, working in BLO, sc 4, bobble, sc 2, bobble, sc 2, bobble, sc 5, join.

Rnd 4: Ch 1, sc 2, invdec, sc 2, invdec, sc 8, join—14 sc.

Rnd 5: Ch 1, sc 3, invdec, sc 1, invdec, sc 6, join—12 sc.

Rnds 6–14: Ch 1, sc around, join.

Change to **B**.

Rnd 15: Ch 1, sc around, join.

Fasten off first Leg. Do not fasten off 2nd Leg. Continue to Body.

Body

Rnd 16: Ch 1, sc 11 around 2nd Leg, skip last st on 2nd Leg, sc in 6th st of first Leg, sc 10 around first Leg, skip last st on 1st Leg, join with a sl st to the first st of 2nd Leg—22 sc.

Rnds 17–18: Ch 1, sc around, join.

Change to **D**.

Use a small length of **B** to sew the 2 unworked stitches inside the Legs shut (this ensures no stuffing will leak out).

Rnd 19: Ch 1, sc around, join.

Rnd 20: Ch 1, working in BLO, sc around, join.

Add armature for the Feet and Legs. To do this, cut a length of wire—I used about 25 inches for this yarn weight and hook size, but if you're using different yarn, you may need to adjust the length. Bend the wire into a "W" shape and push the sides together until it resembles legs. Take one of the outer wires on the W and twist it together with the inner wire next to it, leaving a loop at the bend, or the base of the W (this will be the Foot). Repeat for the other side—the ends of your wires may overlap, but that's okay—just keep twisting them together until you have a length of twisted wire with a loop at each end. Bend the twisted wire into a U shape with each loop at the top, then bend each loop down 90 degrees so that each resembles a flat foot. Insert the loops into the Legs and push them down gently so that they match the contour of the Feet.

Lightly stuff the Feet and Legs around the armature.

Rnds 21–28: Ch 1, sc around, join.

Rnd 29: Ch 1, [sc, invdec] around, sc in remaining st, join—15 sc.

Rnd 30: Ch 1, sc in first st, [invdec] around, join—8 sc.

Change to **C**.

Rnd 31: Ch 1, working in BLO, sc around, join.

Fasten off leaving a long tail for sewing.

Head

With **C** make a magic ring.

Rnd 1: 6 sc in ring, join—6 sc.

Rnd 2: Ch 1, inc around, join—12 sc.

Rnd 3: Ch 1, [sc, inc] around, join—18 sc.

Rnd 4: Ch 1, [sc 2, inc] around, join—24 sc.

Rnd 5: Ch 1, [inc, sc 3] around, join—30 sc.

Rnd 6: Ch 1, [sc 4, inc] around, join—36 sc.

Rnd 7–10: Ch 1, sc around, join.

Rnd 11: Ch 1, [sc 5, inc] around, join—42 sc.

Rnds 12–14: Ch 1, sc around, join.

Attach safety eyes between Rnds 10 and 11, approximately 4 sts apart.

Rnd 15: Ch 1, [sc, invdec] around, join—28 sc.

Rnd 16: Ch 1, invdec around, join—14 sc.

Stuff the Head.

Rnd 17: Ch 1, invdec around, join—7 sc.

Fasten off leaving a long tail for sewing. Sew remaining sts closed. Weave in ends.

At this point, it will be helpful to add the armature for the spine and Head. To do this, cut a length of wire that, when folded in half, is able to extend from the top of the Leg and Foot armature to the top of the Head. Once you have it cut, simply thread the wire under the top of the Leg and Foot armature, until the previous wire is in the middle of the new one and twist the length of new wire tightly around itself. Stop twisting once you get to the neck area, and twist together the ends of any remaining wire, to form a circle. Insert the Head onto this circle.

Sew Head onto the Body, easing in the extra st.

Tunic

With **D**.

With Head facing you, and the toes facing downward, join yarn with a sl st to the unworked BL of Rnd 19 of the Body.

Rnd 1: Ch 1, working in unworked BLO, sc around, join—22 sc.

Rnds 2–7: Ch 1, sc around, join.

Fasten off and weave in end.

Robe

With **F**, leaving a 5" tail.

Row 1: Ch 16, starting in 2nd ch from hook, sc in back bump across, turn—15 sc.

Row 2: Ch 1, sc across, turn.

Row 3: Ch 1, inc, sc 13, inc, turn—17 sc.

Row 4: Ch 1, sc across, turn.

Row 5: Ch 1, inc, sc 15, inc, turn—19 sc.

Row 6: Ch 1, sc across, turn.

Row 7: Ch 1, inc, sc 17, inc, turn—21 sc.

Row 8: Ch 1, sc across, turn.

Row 9: Ch 1, inc, sc 19, inc, turn—23 sc.

Rows 10–21: Ch 1, sc across, turn. At end of last row, do not turn.

Begin working in the rnd for edging.

Rnd 1: Rotate and sc in each row end across the side of the coat, 2 sc in corner, working in underside of chs, sc across, 2 sc in corner, sc in each row end down side, 2 sc in corner, sc across Row, 2 sc in last corner, join.

Change to **B**.

Rnd 2: Ch 1, working in FLO, sc around, join.

Rnd 3: Ch 1, sl st around, join.

Fasten off. Weave in ends.

Arms (Make 2)

With **C**, make a magic ring.
Rnd 1: 6 sc in ring, join—6 sc.
Rnd 2: Ch 1, [sc 2, inc] around, join—8 sc.
Rnd 3: Ch 1, sc around, join.
Rnd 4: Ch 1, bobble, sc around, join.
Rnd 5: Ch 1, sc around, join.
Change to **F**.
Rnds 6–13: Ch 1, sc around, join—8 sc.
Fasten off leaving a tail for sewing.

Cuffs

Rnd 1: Using **B**, join with sl st on Arm between Rnds 5 and 6 where **C** and **F** meet ch 1 and sc in the same st—to do this, insert your hook into a st between rows, yo and pull up a loop, insert hook into the next st between the 2 rows and work a single crochet in that st. Repeat around.
Rnd 2: Sl st around.
Fasten off. Weave in ends. Repeat on other Arm.

Snout

With **E** make a magic ring.
Rnd 1: 6 sc in ring, join—6 sc.
Rnd 2: Ch 1, inc around, join—12 sc.
Begin working in rows.
Rows 3–4: Ch 1, sc across, turn.
Fasten off, leaving a tail for sewing to the Head.

Top of Nose

With **C**, leave a 5"-long tail.
Row 1: Ch 5, starting in 2nd ch from hook, sc in back bump across, turn—4 sc.
Row 2: Ch 1, sc, invdec, sc—3 sc.
Fasten off with a tail for sewing to the snout. Sew the top of the Nose onto the Snout, so that the long end of the top of the Nose is sewn to the end of the Snout. Lightly stuff Snout, and sew it to Head using photo as a guide.

Ears (Make 2)

With **C** make a magic ring.
Rnd 1: 6 sc in ring, join—6 sc.
Rnd 2: Ch 1, inc around, join—12 sc.
Fasten off leaving a tail for sewing to Head. Pinch Ear in half, and, using the yarn tail sew corner together so that it stays folded. Then sew the Ears to the Head underneath Rnd 7, approx. 5 sts away from the eyes.

Crown

With **E**, leave a 5"-long tail.
Row 1: Ch 38, starting in 2nd ch from hook, sc in back bump across, turn—37 sc.
Row 2 (RS): Ch 1, sc, [picot, sc 4, picot] across, turn.
Fasten off. Sew ends together RS facing out. Glue rhinestones to the outside of the crown as pictured. Place on Head.

Sandals (Make 2)

With **G**.
Rnd 1: Ch 6, starting in 2nd ch from hook, sc 4, 3 sc in last ch, rotate to work in underside of chs, sc 3, inc, join—12 sc.
Rnd 2: Ch 1, inc, sc 3, inc 3, sc 3, inc 2, join, turn—18 sc.
Rnd 3: Sl st 5, ch 12, starting in 2nd ch from hook, sl st 11, sl st in remaining sts on Rnd 2, join.
Fasten off, leaving a tail for sewing.

Finishing

Attaching the Robe—Begin by wrapping the coat around the body so that the starting edge (narrower edge) will wrap right around the neck. Create armature for the Arms by cutting a length of wire 12–14" long. Fold each end into the middle, forming a big loop and then wrap each of the smaller ends around the uncut middle of the wire, leaving loops at the ends (these will be the Hands). Insert Arm wire into the Body, through the Body and then out through the Robe again, making sure that each end of the wire is even in length on either side (the wire should stick out between Rnd 28 and 29 of the Body). Then lightly stuff the Arms and place them on the wire, covering it. Sew the ends of the Arms onto the Coat starting under Row 2 and ending around Row 6. Sew the Robe to the torso to stay closed and prevent any wire from being visible between the Robe and Body.

Assembling the Sandals—Weave the tail over to the side of the Sandal opposite the start of the strap (the 12 sl sts) and sew the end of the strap to the side of the Sandal using a whip stitch. Place Sandals on his Feet. Sew in place if desired.

Embroidering the Face—Embroider on the Nose, filling in the V vertically, before sewing a horizonal line across the wide part of the V shape.

Embroider the angry eyelids with **C**, layering 4 stitches.

Embroidering the Robe—Embroider the **A** lines around the edging and cuffs of the Robe.

Weave in remaining ends.

"P. J.! I like that. Do you know I do? Hiss, put it on my luggage."

—Prince John, *Robin Hood* (1973)

Queen of Hearts

Designed by Anna Leyzina

Skill Level: Intermediate

Welcome to Wonderland! Under the rule of the tyrannical Queen of Hearts, everyone is a bit on edge. In fact, the Queen and King of Hearts rule over a kingdom populated by stressed-out playing cards, a Mad Hatter, and at least one white rabbit in quite a rush. The White Rabbit's panic makes sense, as he serves the Queen herself, and she's known for her heated outbursts, demanding attitude, and an unfortunate penchant for threatening to separate subjects from their heads. When the young Alice follows the White Rabbit and inadvertently ventures into the kingdom, she immediately disrupts the Queen's plans. First, she is found painting the Queen's roses! She may have been trying to help one of the playing card soldiers fix their mistake, but it wasn't exactly an auspicious first meeting with the Queen of Hearts. Next, the Queen graciously invites Alice to join a game of croquet. That's when things really go awry. Whether or not Alice is to blame, the Queen of Hearts is delighted to hold her accountable in front of her court. Luckily for Alice, the Queen is easily distracted by a touch of nonsense.

The Queen of Hearts may have a bit of a temper, but her fashion sense is on point! Crochet her red, black, and white ball gown inspired by a deck of playing cards. Top it off with a glorious golden crown. And don't forget her heart scepter! You wouldn't want to upset her carefully curated look!

"Curtsey while you're thinking. It saves time."

—The Queen of Hearts,
Alice in Wonderland (1951)

YARN

Worsted weight (#4 medium) yarn, shown in Lion Brand Basic Stitch Anti Pilling™ (100% acrylic, 185 yd. / 170 m per 3.5 oz. / 100 g skein)

Color A: #400 Red Heather, 1 skein
Color B: #100 White, 1 skein
Color C: #153 Black, 1 skein
Color D: #121 Almond, 1 skein
Color E: #158 Mustard, 1 skein

HOOK

US F (3.75 mm) crochet hook
US D (3.25 mm) crochet hook

NOTIONS

Black size 5 crochet thread
Pair of 8 mm black safety eyes
Small makeup brush
Pink blush
Glue
Toothpick
Stitch markers
Polyester stuffing
Yarn needle
Scissors

FINISHED MEASUREMENTS

Height: 10" / 25 cm
Width: 5" / 12.5 cm

SPECIAL STITCHES

Inc (increase) = Work 2 sc in the next st.

Invdec (invisible single crochet decrease) = Insert hook in front loop only of each of next 2 sts, yo and draw through both sts, yo and draw through 2 loops on hook—1 st decreased.

Picot = Ch 3, sl st in 3rd ch from hook.

Sc2tog (single crochet 2 stitches together) = [Insert hook into next st, yo and draw up a loop] twice, yo and draw through all loops on hook—1 st decreased.

GAUGE

20 sc and 20 rnds = 4 in. / 10 cm in sc

Gauge is not critical for this project. Ensure your stitches are tight so the stuffing won't show through.

NOTES

- Work in continuous rounds unless otherwise indicated.
- When indicated, join at the end of a round with a slip stitch in the first stitch. To join new yarn to a stitch, insert hook in stitch and pull up a loop in indicated color.
- To change colors, work the last yarn over of the previous stitch with the new color. Fasten off previous color unless otherwise indicated.
- If desired, instead of making a magic ring, chain 2 and work indicated stitches in the 2nd chain from the hook.
- Use larger hook unless specified.

Fun Fact
The film *Alice in Wonderland* was in development for over a decade before it went into final production.

Legs (Make 2)

With **A**.

Rnd 1: Ch 5, starting in 2nd ch from hook, sc 2, inc 2, rotate to work in underside of starting ch, inc 2, sc, sc in skipped ch—12 sc.

Rnd 2: Working in BLO, sc around.

Rnd 3: Sl st 2, [invdec] 4 times, sl st 2—8 sts.

Change to **B**.

Rnd 4: Working in BLO, sc 3, sc2tog, sc 3—7 sc.

Rnds 5–10: Sc around.

Rnd 11: Inc, sc 3, inc, sc 2—9 sc.

Rnds 12–14: Sc around.

Sl st in first st. Fasten off and weave in ends. Stuff firmly. Continue to Body.

Body

With back of Legs facing, mark middle st of each inner thigh where Legs will be joined.

With **B** join to the marked st of the Right Leg.

Rnd 15: Ch 3, sc in marked st of Left Leg (this sc is new beginning of rnd), sc around Left Leg, sc into each of the 3 chs, sc in same st on Right Leg as join, sc around Right Leg, sc in underside of each ch—24 sc.

Rnd 16: [Sc 3, inc] 6 times—30 sc.

Rnds 17–18: Sc around.

Rnd 19: [Invdec, sc 3] 6 times—24 sc.

Fasten off. Weave in ends.

Using **A** embroider small Vs to resemble little hearts.

Join **C** in BLO of last st from Rnd 19. Begin to work with 2 colors per rnd. Do not fasten off until indicated.

Rnd 20: Working in BLO, with **C** sc 12, with **A** sc 12.

Rnd 21: Working in BLO, with **C** sc 12, with **A** sc 12.

Rnd 22: With **C** [invdec, sc 2] 3 times, with **A** [sc 2, invdec] 3 times—18 sc.

Rnds 23–25: With **C** sc 9, with **A** sc 9.

Fasten off **A** and **C**. Change to **D**.

Rnd 26: Working in BLO, sc2tog, sc 5, working in both loops [invdec] 2 times, working in BLO, sc 5, sc2tog—14 sc.

Rnd 27: Sc 3, invdec, sc 4, invdec, sc 3—12 sc.

Do not fasten off. Stuff Body firmly. Continue to Head.

Head

With **D**.

Rnd 28: Working in FLO, inc around—24 sc.

Rnd 29: [Sc 3, inc] 6 times—30 sc.

Rnd 30: [Sc 4, inc] 6 times—36 sc.

Rnd 31: [Sc 5, inc] 6 times—42 sc.

Rnd 32: [Sc 6, inc] 6 times—48 sc.

Rnds 33–35: Sc around.

Rnd 36: [Invdec, sc 6] 6 times—42 sc.

Rnds 37–43: Sc around.

Add safety eyes between Rnds 35 and 36, approx. 8 sts apart.

Use black crochet thread to embroider lashes and eyebrows.

Using **D** embroider the nose between Rnds 34 and 35, approx. 2 sts wide.

Using small makeup brush apply blush to create cheeks.

Stuff before the opening becomes too small.

Rnd 44: [Invdec, sc 5] 6 times—36 sc.

Rnd 45: [Invdec, sc 4] 6 times—30 sc.

Rnd 46: [Invdec, sc 3] 6 times—24 sc.

Rnd 47: [Invdec, sc 2] 6 times—18 sc.

Rnd 48: [Invdec, sc] 6 times—12 sc.

Rnd 49: [Invdec] 6 times—6 sc.

Fasten off, leaving a long tail for sewing. Stuff firmly, then sew remaining sts closed and weave in ends.

Skirt

With back of doll facing, turn body upside down. Join **E** in unworked FL of the middle st from Rnd 19 of Body.

Rnd 1: Working in unworked FLO, [sc 3, inc] 6 times—30 sc.

Rnds 2–3: Sc around.

Change to **C**.

Rnd 4: Sc around.

Rnd 5: [Sc 4, inc] 6 times—36 sc.

Change to **E**.

Rnds 6–8: Sc around.

Change to **C**.

Rnd 9: [Sc 5, inc] 6 times—42 sc.

Rnd 10: Sc around.

Change to **E**.

Rnds 11–13: Sc around.

Fasten off. Weave in ends.

Bustle

With front of doll facing, turn body upside down. Join **A** in unworked FL of **C** st at middle of front on Rnd 20.

Begin to work with 2 colors per row. Do not fasten off until indicated.

Row 1: Working in unused FLO, with **A** [sc, inc] 6 times, with **C** [inc, sc] 6 times, turn—36 sc.

Row 2: With **C**, ch 1, sc2tog, sc 16, with **A** sc 16, sc2tog, ch 1, turn—34 sc.

Row 3: With **A**, ch 1, sc 17, with **C** sc 17, turn.

Row 4: With **C**, ch 1, sc 17, with **A** sc 17, turn.

Row 5: With **A**, ch 1, sc2tog, sc 15, with **C** sc 15, sc2tog, turn—32 sc.

Row 6: With **C**, ch 1, sc 16, with **A** sc 16, turn.

Row 7: With **A**, ch 1, sc 16, with **C** sc 16, turn.

Row 8: With **C**, ch 1, sc2tog, sc 14, with **A** sc 14, sc2tog, turn—30 sc.

Row 9: With **A**, ch 1, sc 15, with **C** sc 15, turn.

Row 10: With **C**, ch 1, sc 15, with **A** sc 15, turn.

Row 11: With **A**, ch 1, sc2tog, sc 13, with **C** sc 13, sc2tog, turn—sc.

Row 12: With **C**, ch 1, sc 14, with **A** sc 14.

Fasten off. Weave in ends.

Join **B** in side of first **A** st in Row 1, sc evenly down ends of rows, sc across Row 12, sc evenly up ends of rows to Bustle. Fasten off. Weave in ends.

Right Arm

With **D** make a magic ring.

Rnd 1: 4 sc into ring—4 sc.

Rnd 2: [Sc, inc] twice—6 sc.

Rnds 3–4: Sc around.

Change to **A**.

Rnd 5: Sc around.

Rnd 6: Working into BLO, sc around.

Rnd 7: Sc around.

Rnd 8: Inc, sc 5—7 sc.

Rnds 9–10: Sc around.

Rnd 11: Sc 3, inc, sc 3—8 sc.

Rnds 12–13: Sc around.

Fasten off, leaving a long tail. Stuff the Arm, then squeeze opening together, with 4 sts side by side. Sew the sides together. Do not trim tail.

Cuff

Turn Arm upside down and join **C** to any unworked FL on Rnd 5.

Rnd 1: Working in unworked FLO, [sc, inc] 3 times—9 sc.

Rnd 2: Working into BLO, sc around.

Fasten off and weave in ends.

Left Arm

Follow instructions for Right Arm using **C** for **A** and **A** for **C**.

Collar

With **B**.

Row 1: Ch 11, starting in 4th ch from hook (skipped chs do not count as st), dc 2, hdc 2, sc 2, sl st 2, turn—8 sts.

Row 2: Ch 1, sl st 2, sc 2, hdc 2, dc 2, turn.

Row 3: Ch 3 (*does not count as st*), dc 2, hdc 2, sc, 2, sl st 2, turn.

Rows 4–17: Repeat Rows 2 and 3.

Fasten off, leaving a long tail.

Hair

With **C** make a magic ring.

Rnd 1: 6 sc into ring—6 sc.

Rnd 2: Inc around—12 sc.

Rnd 3: [Sc, inc] 6 times—18 sc.

Rnd 4: Working into BLO, [sc 2, inc] 6 times—24 sc.

Rnd 5: [Sc 3, inc] 6 times—30 sc.

Rnd 6: [Sc 4, inc] 6 times—36 sc.

Rnd 7: [Sc 5, inc] 6 times—42 sc.

Rnds 8–13: Sc around.

Rnd 14: Sl st in first st, ch 3 (counts as first st), dc 18, hdc, sc, sl st, sc, hdc, dc 18, join.

Fasten off, leaving a long tail.

Bun

Join **C** in center back unworked FL on Rnd 3 of Hair.

Rnd 1: Working in unworked FLO, [sc 2, inc] 6 times—24 sc.

Rnds 2–4: Sc around.

Rnd 5: [Sc 2, invdec] 6 times—18 sc.

Rnd 6: [Sc, invdec] 6 times—12 sc.

Rnd 7: [Invdec] 6 times—6 sc.

Stuff before moving to the next round.

Rnd 8: Working into FLO, inc around—12 sc.

Rnds 9–10: Sc around.

Rnd 11: [Invdec] 6 times—6 sc.

Fasten off, leaving a long tail for sewing. Stuff firmly, then sew remaining sts closed and weave in ends.

Ribbon

With **A** ch 22. Fasten off, tie a knot after last ch, and trim off excess ends. Use a little dab of craft or fabric glue to keep knots from unraveling. Wrap the ch between 2 Buns, secure with a double knot.

Left Ear

With **D** and smaller hook.

Row 1: Ch 3, 3 sc in 2nd ch from hook, (sc, ch 1, sl st) in last ch.

Fasten off, leaving a long tail.

Right Ear

With **D** and smaller hook.

Row 1: Ch 3, sc in 2nd ch from hook, (3 sc, ch 1, sl st) in last ch.

Fasten off, leaving a long tail.

Earrings (Make 2)

With **D** and smaller hook.

Row 1: Ch 3, hdc into 3rd ch from hook.

Fasten off leaving a tail.

Crown

With **E** and smaller hook.

Rnd 1: Ch 11, starting in 2nd ch from hook, sc 10, join in first sc to form a ring—10 sc.

Rnd 2: Ch 1, [(sc, picot, sc) in next st, skip 1 st] 5 times, join.

Fasten off and weave in ends. Use starting tail to close the gap in the foundation.

Heart (Make 2)

With **A** and smaller hook, make a magic ring.

Rnd 1 (RS): (Ch 3, dc 2, hdc, sc, ch 2, sc, hdc, dc 2, ch 3, sl st) into ring.

Fasten off and weave in ends. Make another Heart.

Glue WS of the Hearts together (RS facing out), placing a toothpick in between.

Finishing

Sew Hair securely to the top of the Head. Stitch 3 lines at the top of the hairline to mimic 3 strands of hair.

Sew the Collar to the unworked FL on Rnd 25 of Body.

Sew Arms to the sides of the Body, right under the Collar.

Sew each Earring to the front of each Ear. Sew each Ear to the corresponding side of the Head, right under the Hair, between Rnds 33–36.

Sew Crown to the Head using **C**.

Placing toothpick directly through one of the Hands, secure in place with glue.

JOURNEYS THROUGH BOOKLAND
SYLVESTER
VOLUME X
JOURNEYS THROUGH BOOKLAND
SYLVESTER
VOLUME IV

Hans

Designed by Lee Sartori

Skill Level: Easy

Prince Hans of the Southern Isles is ambitious. He has dreams of ruling one day, just like his royal parents. There is one problem: Prince Hans is the thirteenth child in his family and so far removed from the royal accession that he may as well be a commoner. One way to gain the power and recognition that he so desperately seeks is to marry into another royal family with more upward advancement. Luckily for Hans, a royal event in neighboring Arendelle presents him with an opportunity to woo either of the two beautiful princesses living there. Setting his sights on Princess Anna, Hans turns on the charm. With twelve older brothers, Hans grew up feeling practically invisible, and Anna can relate. Plus, Hans knows how to play the part of an observant and chivalrous prince—everything that Anna has been waiting for. After securing Anna's heart, there is only one thing left in his way. Or one person, we should say. Anna's sister, Queen Elsa, has to go and by any means necessary.

Though some expect villains to be draped in dark-colored clothing and accessories, Prince Hans of the Southern Isles is typically dressed in light and bright colors. Highly polished boots and a formal naval jacket make Hans look smart and capable—but capable of what, you may ask? Don't let the friendly uniform in this crochet pattern fool you. Hans is definitely a foe of the worst kind.

"You're no match for Elsa. I, on the other hand, am the hero who's going to save Arendelle from destruction."

—Hans, *Frozen* (2013)

YARN

Worsted weight (#4 medium) yarn, shown in Lion Brand Basic Stitch Anti Pilling™ (100% acrylic, 185 yd. / 170 m per 3.5 oz. / 100 g skein)

Color A: #100 White, 1 skein
Color B: #153 Black, 1 skein
Color C: #406N Deep Denim Heather, 1 skein
Color D: #110AW Stonewash, 1 skein
Color E: #121L Almond, 1 skein
Color F: #134U Honey, 1 skein
Color G: #112S Deco Rose, 1 skein
Color H: #158L Mustard, 1 skein

HOOK

US D (3.25 mm) crochet hook

NOTIONS

Pair of 9 mm black safety eyes
Black felt
Small amount of plastic mesh
Glue
Stitch markers
Polyester stuffing
Yarn needle
Scissors

FINISHED MEASUREMENTS

Height: 13" / 32.5 cm
Width: 8" / 20 cm

SPECIAL STITCHES

Inc (increase) = Work 2 sc in the next st.

Invdec (invisible single crochet decrease) = Insert hook in front loop only of each of next 2 sts, yo and draw through both sts, yo and draw through 2 loops on hook—1 st decreased.

Popcorn (popcorn stitch) = Work 5 dc in next st, drop loop on hook, insert hook from front to back in first dc made, place dropped loop on hook and draw through dc.

Sc2tog (single crochet 2 together) = [Insert hook in next st, yo and draw up a loop] twice, yo and draw through all loops on hook—1 st decreased.

GAUGE

28 sc and 28 rnds = 4 in. / 10 cm in sc

Gauge is not critical for this project. Ensure your stitches are tight so the stuffing won't show through.

NOTES

- Work in continuous rounds unless otherwise indicated.
- When indicated, join at the end of a round with a slip stitch in the first stitch. To join new yarn to a stitch, insert hook in stitch and pull up a loop in indicated color.
- To change colors, work the last yarn over of the previous stitch with the new color. Fasten off previous color unless otherwise indicated.
- If desired, instead of making a magic ring, chain 2 and work indicated stitches in the 2nd chain from the hook.

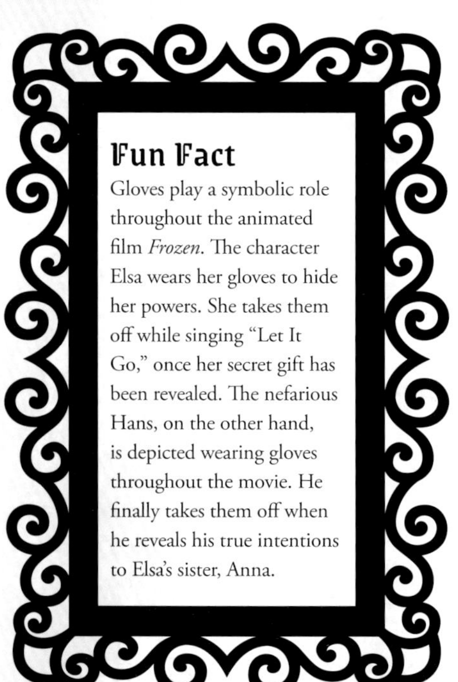

Fun Fact

Gloves play a symbolic role throughout the animated film *Frozen*. The character Elsa wears her gloves to hide her powers. She takes them off while singing "Let It Go," once her secret gift has been revealed. The nefarious Hans, on the other hand, is depicted wearing gloves throughout the movie. He finally takes them off when he reveals his true intentions to Elsa's sister, Anna.

Arms (Make 2)

With **A**, make a magic ring.

Rnd 1: 6 sc in ring—6 sc.

Rnd 2: Inc around—12 sc.

Rnds 3–4: Sc around.

Rnd 5: Popcorn, sc 11.

Rnds 6–7: Sc around.

Rnd 8: [Invdec, sc 2] around, join—9 sc.

Rnd 9: Sc around.

Rnd 10: [Sc, inc, sc] around—12 sc.

Rnds 11–15: Sc around.

Rnd 16: [Inc, sc 3] around—15 sc.

Rnds 17–26: Sc around.

Fasten off and weave in ends. Stuff Arm lightly. Set aside to join to Body.

Cuffs (Make 2)

With **B**.

Row 1: Ch 6, starting in 2nd ch from hook sc across, turn—5 sc.

Rows 2–15: Ch 1, sc across, turn.

Fasten off, leaving a long tail for sewing. Wrap around wrist of Arm and sew closed. Weave in ends.

Boot Soles (Make 4)

With **B**.

Rnd 1: Ch 7, starting in 2nd ch from hook, sc 5, 3 sc in last ch, rotate to work on underside of starting ch, sc 5, 3 sc in skipped ch—16 sc.

Rnd 2: *Sc 5, inc 3; repeat from * around—22 sc.

Rnd 3: *Sc 5, [inc, sc] 3 times; repeat from * around—28 sc.

Fasten off 1st Sole. Do not fasten off 2nd Sole. Place 1st Sole on top of plastic mesh and trace shape. Cut out plastic and insert between 2 Soles.

Rnd 4 (joining): With 2 Soles held together and plastic inserted between them, sc around through both thicknesses to join—28 sc.

Continue to Boot.

Boots (Make 2)

Continuing with **B**.

Rnd 1: Sc 5, [invdec, sc] 3 times, sc 14—25 sc.

Rnd 2: Sc 5, [invdec] 5 times, sc 10—20 sc.

Rnd 3: Sc 4, [invdec] 3 times, sc 10—17 sc.

Rnd 4: Sc 3, [invdec] 3 times, sc 8—14 sc.

Rnds 5–11: Sc around.

Fasten off. Stuff Boot. Continue to Leg.

Legs (Make 2)

Join **C** to sc at back of heel of Boot in BLO.

Rnd 1: Ch 1, working in BLO sc around, join—14 sc.

Rnd 2: Ch 1, inc, sc around, join—15 sc.

Rnds 3–6: Ch 1, sc around, join.

Rnd 7: Ch 1, [sc 2, inc, sc 2] around, join—18 sc.

Rnds 8–15: Ch 1, sc around, join.

Fasten off 1st Leg, do not fasten off 2nd Leg. Using st markers, mark center st of inner thigh of each Leg where Legs will meet.

Rnd 16 (joining): Ch 1, sc around to first marked st, sc in marked st, sc in marked st on 1st Leg, sc around 1st Leg, sc in remaining sts on 2nd Leg, join—36 sc.

Rnd 17: Ch 1, sc around, join.

Rnd 18: Ch 1, [inc, sc 5] around, join—42 sc.

Rnds 19–26: Ch 1, sc around.

Fasten off. Continue to Body.

Body

Join **B** to sc at back of Legs in BLO.

Rnd 1: Ch 1, working in BLO sc around, join—42 sc.

Rnd 2: Ch 1, sc around, join.

Change to **D**.

Rnd 3: Ch 1, sc around, join.

Rnd 4: Ch 1 tightly, sc around, do not join.

Rnds 5–16: Sc around.

Fold last of rnd of Arms in half, with 7 pairs of sts and 1 extra st that will be skipped. Using st markers, mark 7 sts on either side of Body (st marker in first and 7th st) for joining Arms. Leave 14 sts between markers for front of Body, and 14 sts for the back of the Body. Hold Arms in line with Body, thumbs facing forward, to join in next rnd.

Rnd 17: Sc around Body to marker, sc through 7 pairs of sts at top of first Arm and 7 marked sts on Body, sc around Body to next marker, sc through 7 pairs of sts at top of 2nd Arm and 7 marked sts on Body, sc in remaining sts on Body, join—42 sc.

Rnd 18: [Invdec, sc 5] around—36 sc.

Rnd 19: [Sc 2, invdec, sc 2] around—30 sc.

Rnd 20: [Invdec, sc 3] around—24 sc.

Rnd 21: Working in BLO [sc, sc2tog, sc] around, join—18 sc.

Fasten off. Stuff Body. Continue to Neck.

Neck

Join **E** to sc at back of Body in BLO.

Rnd 1: Ch 1, working in BLO sc around, join—18 sc.

Rnds 2–3: Ch 1, sc around, join.

Rnd 4: Ch 1, inc around, join—36 sc.

Rnd 5: Ch 1, [inc, sc 5] around, join—42 sc.

Rnd 6: Ch 1 tightly, sc around, do not join.

Rnds 7–18: Sc around.

Add safety eyes between Rnds 13 and 14, approximately 8 sts apart. Using a length of **E**, embroider nose between Rnds 11 and 12 over 3 sts. Using a length of **F**, add eyebrows above eyes.

Rnd 19: [Invdec, sc 5] around—36 sc.

Stuff Head, continue stuffing as work progresses.

Rnd 20: [Sc 2, invdec, sc 2] around—30 sc.

Rnd 21: [Invdec, sc 3] around—24 sc.

Rnd 22: [Sc, invdec, sc] around—18 sc.

Rnd 23: [Invdec, sc] around—12 sc.

Rnd 24: Invdec around—6 sc.

Fasten off, leaving a long tail for sewing. Sew remaining 6 sts closed. Weave in end.

Shirt Collar (Make 2)

With **D**.

Row 1: Ch 5, starting in 2nd ch from hook sc, hdc, dc, tr.

Fasten off, leaving a long tail for sewing. Sew to center 6 unworked FL at beginning of Neck. Weave in ends.

Gold Belt Buttons (Make 2)

With **H** make a magic ring.

Rnd 1: 4 sc in ring, join—4 sc.

Fasten off, leaving a long tail for sewing. Sew to first 2 rnds of Body.

Coat

With **A**.

Row 1: Ch 22, starting in 2nd ch from hook sc across, turn—21 sc.

Rows 2–12: Ch 1, sc across, turn.

Row 13: Ch 1, sc 7, turn, leaving remaining sts unworked—7 sc.

Rows 14–32 (1st Front Panel): Ch 1, sc 7, turn.

Fasten off.

Skip next 7 unworked sts of Row 12 and join in next st.

Rows 1–20 (2nd Front Panel): Ch 1, sc 7, turn.

Fasten off, leaving a long tail for sewing. Fold piece in half with Rows 1–12 as back panel, with 2 Front Panels on top. Sew underarm seam from bottom hem up 6 rows toward armpit, leaving remaining rows unsewn for arm.

Border: Join to bottom of left Front Panel, ch 1, sc 7 across, working in underside of chs of Row 1, sc 21, working across right Front Panel, sc 7, ch 1, sc 19 across row ends of panel up to neck, sc 7 on back of neck, sc 19 down row ends of panel, ch 1, join—80 sc.

Fasten off.

Sleeve edge: Join to bottom edge of arm opening, ch 1, sc 20 evenly around arm opening, join—20 sc.

Fasten off.

Repeat for opposite sleeve edge. Weave in ends.

Coat Collar

With **B**, leaving a long tail at start for sewing.

Row 1: Ch 16, starting in 2nd ch from hook sc across, turn—15 sc.

Row 2: Ch 1, sc, hdc, dc, tr 9, dc, hdc, sc.

Fasten off, weave in end. Using starting tail, sew to back 15 sts of Coat around neck. Weave in end.

Epaulettes (Make 2)

With **B** leaving a long tail at start for sewing.

Row 1: Ch 7, starting in 2nd ch from hook sc across, turn—6 sc.

Row 2: Ch 1, sc 4, sc2tog, turn—5 sc.

Row 3: Ch 1, sc2tog, sc 3, turn—4 sc.

Row 4: Ch 1, sc 2, sc2tog, turn—3 sc.

Row 5: Ch 1, sc2tog, sc, turn—2 sc.

Row 6: Ch 1, sc2tog, turn—1 sc.

Row 7: Ch 1, sc.

Fasten off, leaving a long tail for sewing. Using starting tail, sew 6 starting chs to side edge of Coat below Collar. Using finishing tail, secure tip of Epaulette to edge of Coat shoulder. Weave in ends.

Medal

With **H** and leaving a long tail, make a magic ring.

Rnd 1: 4 sc in ring, join, ch 14—4 sc, 14 chs.

Fasten off, leaving a long tail for sewing. Using starting tail, ch 4. Sew Medal to front of Coat with ch 14 secured to top of shoulder. Weave in ends.

Coattail

With **A**.

Row 1: Ch 2, 3 sc in 2nd ch from hook, turn—3 sc.

Row 2: Ch 1, inc across, turn—6 sc.

Row 3: Ch 1, [inc, sc] across, turn—9 sc.

Row 4: Ch 1, [inc, sc 2] across, turn—12 sc.

Row 5: Ch 1, [inc, sc 3] across, turn—15 sc.

Row 6: Ch 1, [inc, sc 4] across, turn—18 sc.

Row 7: Ch 1, [inc, sc 5] across, turn—21 sc.

Row 8: Ch 1, [inc, sc 6] across, turn—24 sc.

Row 9: Ch 1, [inc, sc 7] across, turn—27 sc.

Row 10: Ch 1, [inc, sc 8] across, turn—30 sc.

Row 11: Ch 1, [inc, sc 9] across, turn—33 sc.
Row 12: Ch 1, [inc, sc 10] across, do not turn—36 sc.
Row 13: Ch 1, rotate to work 24 sc evenly across row ends, turn—24 sc.
Rows 14–23: Ch 1, sc across, turn.
Fasten off, leaving a long tail for sewing. Sew to back 24 sts of Coat. Weave in ends.

Neck Tie

With **G**.
Row 1: Ch 12, starting in 2nd ch from hook sc across—11 sc.
Fasten off, weave in ends. Using a length of **G**, fold Neck Tie in half lengthwise and tie a loop around the middle. Use ends to sew between Shirt Collar.

Hair

With **F** make a magic ring.
Rnd 1: 6 sc in ring—6 sc.
Rnd 2: Inc around—12 sc.
Rnd 3: [Inc, sc] around—18 sc.
Rnd 4: [Sc, inc, sc] around—24 sc.
Rnd 5: [Inc, sc 3] around—30 sc.
Rnd 6: [Sc 2, inc, 2 sc] around—36 sc.
Rnd 7: [Inc, sc 5] around—42 sc.
Rnds 8–11: Sc around.
Rnd 12: [Sc 3, inc, sc 3] around—48 sc.
Rnds 13–15: Sc around.
Fasten off, leaving a long tail for sewing. Sew to top of Head. Weave in end.

Hair Strand

With **F**.
Row 1: *Ch 12, starting in 4th ch from hook, dc 9; repeat from * 9 more times—10 strands of hair.
Fasten off, leaving a long tail for sewing. Sew around top of Head with 5 strands on either side to create a center part. Weave in ends.

Ears (Make 2)

With **E** make a magic ring.
Rnd 1: 6 sc in ring—6 sc.
Fasten off, leaving a long tail for sewing. Sew Ear to either side of Head in front of Hair. Weave in ends.

Sideburns (Make 2)

With **F**.
Row 1: Ch 7, starting in 2nd ch from hook sc across—6 sc.
Fasten off, leaving a long tail for sewing. Sew to sides of face in front of Ears. Weave in ends.

Finishing

Using black felt, cut 4 small circles to act as shirt buttons and glue to front of shirt.

Part 2

Plotters and Schemers

Captain Hook

Designed by Valérie Prieur-Côté

Skill Level: Intermediate

Being a pirate captain in Never Land comes with plenty of perks. A crew of loyal sailors, the wide-open sea, and treasure! If only it weren't for those blasted Lost Boys, led by the persistent Peter Pan. If it weren't for Pan, Captain Hook wouldn't have a crocodile chasing him, and he wouldn't be listening for the sound of a ticking clock every time he steps out on deck of *The Jolly Roger*. With the help of his trusty boatswain, Mr. Smee, Captain Hook has changed course from hunting treasure to seeking revenge against Pan. Now, if that day were to come, it would be a lovely new feather in his captain's cap indeed.

Captain Hook may seem dangerous like a menacing swashbuckler, but don't worry! Our amigurumi version of the pirate captain features a crocheted sword and hook—a safer way to capture a pirate's flair. Paired with his signature cap and his dapper coat, this crochet Captain Hook is *all* style.

"I'll get you for this, Pan, if it's the last thing I do!"

—Captain Hook, *Peter Pan* (1953)

YARN

Worsted weight (#4 medium) yarn, shown in WeCrochet Swish (100% fine superwash merino wool, 110 yd. / 100 m per 1.75 oz. / 50 g ball)

Color A: Black, 1 ball
Color B: White, 1 ball
Color C: Crush, 1 ball
Color D: Shortbread, 1 ball
Color E: Dove Heather, 1 ball
Color F: Phoenix, 1 ball
Color G: Dijon, 1 ball
Color H: Cider, 1 ball

HOOK

US D (3.25 mm) crochet hook
US C (2.75 mm) crochet hook

NOTIONS

Pair of 6 mm black safety eyes
White feather
Glue
Stitch markers
Polyester stuffing
Yarn needle
Scissors

FINISHED MEASUREMENTS

Height: 9" / 22.5 cm
Width: 4" / 10 cm

GAUGE

28 sc and 28 rnds = 4 in. / 10 cm in sc

Gauge is not critical for this project. Ensure your stitches are tight so the stuffing won't show through.

SPECIAL STITCHES

Inc (increase) = Work 2 sc in next st.

Invdec (invisible single crochet decrease) = Insert hook in front loop only of each of next 2 sts, yo and draw through both sts, yo and draw through 2 loops on hook—1 st decreased.

Hdc-invdec (invisible half double crochet decrease) = Yo, insert hook in front loop only of each of next 2 sts, yo and draw through both sts, yo and draw through all loops on hook—1 st decreased.

Standing sc (standing sc) = With slipknot on hook, insert hook in indicated st, yo and draw up a loop, yo and draw through 2 loops on hook.

Bobble (bobble stitch) = [Yo, insert hook into st, yo and draw up a loop, yo and draw through 2 loops on hook] 4 times, yo and draw through all loops on hook.

Fsc (foundation single crochet) = With slipknot on hook, ch 2. Insert hook into 2nd ch from hook, yo and draw up a loop, yo and draw through 1 loop on hook *(foundation made)*, yo and draw through 2 loops on hook—1 Fsc completed. *Insert hook under the 2 loops of the foundation of previous Fsc, yo and draw up a loop, yo and draw through 1 loop on hook *(foundation made)*, yo and draw through 2 loops on hook—Fsc completed. Repeat from * until required number of Fsc are made.

Fhdc (foundation half double crochet) = With slipknot on hook, ch 2. Yo, insert hook into 2nd ch from hook, yo and draw up a loop, yo and draw through 1 loop on hook *(foundation made)*, yo and draw through 3 loops on hook—1 Fhdc completed. *Yo, insert hook under the 2 loops of the foundation of previous Fhdc, yo and draw up a loop, yo and draw through 1 loop on hook *(foundation made)*, yo and draw through 3 loops on hook—Fhdc completed. Repeat from * until required number of Fhdc are made.

NOTES

- Use smaller hook unless indicated otherwise.
- Work in continuous rounds unless otherwise indicated.
- When indicated, join at the end of a round with a slip stitch in the first stitch. To join new yarn to a stitch, insert hook in stitch and pull up a loop in indicated color.
- To change colors, work the last yarn over of the previous stitch with the new color. Fasten off previous color unless otherwise indicated.
- If desired, instead of making a magic ring, chain 2 and work indicated stitches in the 2nd chain from the hook.

Arm

With **D** make a magic ring.
Rnd 1: 4 sc in ring—4 sc.
Rnd 2: [Sc, inc] around—6 sc.
Rnd 3: [Sc 2, inc] around—8 sc.
Rnd 4: Sc around.
Rnd 5: Sc, bobble, sc 6.
Rnds 6–7: Sc around.
Change to **B**.
Rnd 8: Working in BLO, sc around.
Rnds 9–18: Sc around.
Do not stuff.
Rnd 19: Ch 1, fold opening in half, working through both thicknesses, sc across—4 sc.
Fasten off.

Arm with Hook

With **E** make a magic ring.
Rnd 1: 4 sc in ring—4 sc.
Rnd 2: Inc around—8 sc.
Rnd 3: Sc around.
Change to **B**.
Rnd 4: Working in BLO, sc around.
Rnds 5–13: Sc around.
Do not stuff.
Rnd 14: Ch 1, fold opening in half, working through both thicknesses, sc across—4 sc.
Fasten off.

Hook

With **E**, ch 11, starting in 2nd ch from hook, sc 4, invdec, sc 4—9 sc.
Fasten off, leaving a long tail.
Sew Hook to middle of Arm end with tail.

Nose

With **D** make a magic ring.
Rnd 1: 4 sc in ring—4 sc.
Rnd 2: Inc around—8 sc.
Rnd 3: Sc around.
Rnd 4: Sc 3, inc 2, sc 3—10 sc.
Rnd 5: Sc around.
Row 6: Ch 1, turn, sc 6, leaving remaining sts unworked—6 sc.
Fasten off, leaving a long tail to sew.

Moustache (Make 2)

With **A**, ch 9, starting in 2nd ch from hook, sl st 4, sc 2, hdc 2—8 sts.
Fasten off, leaving a long tail to sew.

Legs (Make 2)

With **A**.
Rnd 1: Ch 8, starting in 2nd ch from the hook, sc 6, 4 sc in last ch, working in the underside of chs, sc 5, 3 sc in last ch—18 sc.
Rnd 2: Sc 6, inc 4, sc 6, inc 2—24 sc.
Rnd 3: Working in BLO, sc around.
Rnd 4: Sc around.
Rnd 5: Sc 5, [invdec] twice, hdc-invdec, [invdec] twice, sc 9—19 sts.
Rnd 6: Sc 3, [invdec] 5 times, sc 6—14 sc.
Change to **B**.
Rnd 7: Working in BLO, sc 5, invdec, sc 7—13 sc.
Rnd 8: Sc 11, invdec—12 sc.
Rnds 9–15: Sc around.
Change to **C**.
Rnd 16: Working in FLO, sc 3, inc, sc 4, inc, sc 3—14 sc.

Rnds 17–24: Sc around.

Fasten off first Leg. Do not fasten off 2nd Leg. If necessary, work additional sc to shift beginning of round to middle of Leg's inner side. Stuff Legs. Continue to Body.

Body and Head

Hold Legs aligned, with toes facing same direction, to join in next rnd.

Rnd 1: Ch 1, sc around first Leg, sc in ch, sc around 2nd Leg, sc in underside of ch—30 sc.

Rnds 2–6: Sc around.

If needed, work additional sc to shift beginning of rnd to middle of back.

Change to **B**.

Rnd 7: Working in BLO, sc around.

Rnds 8-16: Sc around.

Rnd 17: [Sc 3, invdec] around—24 sc.

Rnd 18: [Sc 4, invdec] around—20 sc.

Rnd 19: Sc around.

Hold Arms in line with Body to join in next rnd.

Rnd 20: Sc around Body, working through both Arm and Body sts to join—20 sc.

Rnd 21: [Sc 3, invdec] around—16 sc.

Rnd 22: [Sc 2, invdec] around—12 sc.

Start stuffing.

Change to **D**.

Rnd 23: Working in BLO, sc around.

Rnd 24: [Invdec] 6 times—6 sc.

Rnd 25: Inc around—12 sc.

Rnd 26: [Sc, inc] around—18 sc.

Rnd 27: [Sc 2, inc] around—24 sc.

Rnd 28: Sc, inc, [sc 3, inc] 5 times, sc 2—30 sc.

Rnd 29: [Sc 4, inc] around—36 sc.

Rnds 30–42: Sc around.

Rnd 43: [Sc 4, invdec] around—30 sc.

Place eyes between the Rnds 36 and 37, 5–6 stitches apart.

Sew Nose on Head, with top row of Nose around Rnd 34 and centered between eyes. Stuff Nose slightly

Sew on Moustache under Nose.

Rnd 44: Sc, invdec, [sc 3, invdec] 5 times, sc 2—24 sc.

Rnd 45: [Sc 2, invdec] around—18 sc

Rnd 46: [Sc, invdec] around—12 sc

Stuff Head.

Rnd 47: Invdec around—6 sc.

Fasten off, leaving a long tail for sewing. Sew remaining 6 sts closed. Weave in ends.

Shoe Detail (Make 2)

With **A**, in unworked FL on 3 center sts of Shoe, join yarn in FL of rightmost st.

Row 1: Working in unworked FLO, sc 3, turn—3 sc.

Row 2: Ch 1, inc, sc, inc, turn—5 sc.

Row 3: Ch 1, sc across.

Fasten off and weave ends in.

Shoe Buckles (Make 2)

With **G**, ch 4. Fasten off, leaving a tail for sewing.

Sew to Shoes using photo as a guide.

Face Details

Sew **B** on the side of the eyes.

Using **A**, make 2 angry eyebrows.

Coat

With **F** and 3.25 mm hook.

Row 1: Fsc 40, turn—40 sts.

Rows 2–5: Ch 1, sc across, turn.

Row 6: Ch 1, sc 4, [invdec, sc 8] 3 times, invdec, sc 4, turn—36 sc.

Row 7: Ch 1, sc across, turn.

Row 8: Ch 1, sc 4, [invdec, sc 7] 3 times, invdec, sc 3, turn—32 sc.

Row 9: Ch 1, sc across, turn.

Row 10: Ch 1, sc 3, [invdec, sc 6] 3 times, invdec, sc 3, turn—28 sc.

Row 11: Ch 1, sc across, turn.

Row 12: Ch 1, sc 3, [invdec, sc 5] 3 times, invdec, sc 2, turn—24 sc.

Row 13: Ch 1, sc 2, [invdec, sc 4] 3 times, invdec, sc 2, turn—20 sc.

Row 14–19: Ch 1, sc across, turn.

Row 20: Ch 1, sc 3, ch 4, skip 4 sc *(sleeve opening made)*, sc 6, ch 4, skip 4 sc *(sleeve opening made)*, sc 3, turn—12 sc, 8 chs.

Row 21: Ch 1, working in sc and chs across, [sc 3, invdec] across—16 sc.

Fasten off.

Border

Join **G** at top of left opening, hdc evenly down Coat. Fasten off. Repeat on opposite side. Do not weave in ends.

Sleeves (Make 2)

Rnd 1: Join **F** with standing sc on Coat in first skipped st of Rnd 19, sc 3, sc in side between row and chs, sc in underside of chs, sc in side between chs and first sc—10 sc.
Rnds 2–17: Sc around.
Fasten off. Fold up last 4 rows to create cuff. Use yarn tail to secure.
Repeat on other armhole.
Place Coat on doll. Using tail from Border, sew together each side of the Border, starting at the collar and ending approximately where the pants start on the doll. Fasten off and weave in ends.

Ruffles

With **B**, join in unworked FL at wrists of Arms, inc in each FLO around. Fasten off. Repeat on the other Arm. Weave in ends.

Ascot

Row 1: Ch 17, starting in 2nd ch from hook, hdc across, turn—16 hdc.
Rows 2–3: Ch 1, hdc across, turn.
Fasten off, leaving a long tail.
Fold the rectangle to form a Z. Use tail to sew in place at same rnd as color change from Body to Head.

Hair

With **A** and 3.25 mm hook.
Row 1: Ch 26, starting in 2nd ch from hook 2 hdc in next 11 chs, hdc 14, turn—36 hdc.
Row 2: Ch 1, working in FLO, hdc 14, leaving remaining sts unworked, ch 12, turn—14 hdc, 12 chs.
Row 3: Starting in 2nd ch from hook, 2 hdc in next ch, hdc 10, continuing on previous row in BLO, hdc 14, turn—26 hdc.
Repeat Rows 2–3 an additional 7 times.
Fasten off, leaving a long tail.
Pass tail through ends of rows at straight edge and pull on the tail to form a U shape. Sew Wig on Head.

Hat

With **C** and 3.25 mm hook, make a magic ring.
Rnd 1: 6 sc in ring—6 sc.
Rnd 2: Inc around—12 sc.
Rnd 3: [Sc, inc] around—18 sc.
Rnd 4: [Sc 2, inc] around—24 sc.
Rnd 5: [Sc 3, inc] around—30 sc.
Rnd 6: [Sc 4, inc] around—36 sc.
Rnd 7: Working in BLO, sc around.
Rnds 8–9: Sc around.
Rnd 10: Working in FLO, sc around.
Rnd 11: [Sc 5, inc] around—42 sc.
Rnd 12: [Sc 6, inc] around—48 sc.
Begin working in turned rows for left side of Hat.
Row 1: Sc 12, turn leaving remaining sts unworked—12 sc.
Row 2: Ch 1, invdec, sc 8, invdec, turn—10 sc.
Row 3: Ch 1, invdec, sc 6, invdec, turn—8 sc.
Row 4: Ch 1, invdec, sc 4, invdec, turn—6 sc.
Fasten off.
Skip next 9 unworked sc on Rnd 12. Join in next sc.
Rnd 1: Sc 14, turn, leaving remaining sts unworked—14 sc.
Row 2: Ch 1, sc across, turn.
Row 3: Ch 1, invdec, sc 10, invdec, turn—12 sc.
Row 4: Ch 1, invdec, sc 8, invdec, turn—10 sc.
Row 5: Ch 1, invdec, sc 6, invdec, turn—8 sc.
Row 6: Ch 1, sc across, turn.
Row 7: Ch 1, invdec, sc 4, invdec, turn—6 sc.
Row 8: Ch 1, sc, hdc, dc 2, hdc, sc, turn.
Edging: Sc evenly around Hat, working invdec where base meets sides to help folds stay upright.
Fasten off and weave in ends.
Glue feather on side of Hat.

Sword Sheath

With **H** and 3.25 mm hook, Fhdc 45. Fasten off leaving a small tail.
With **H** make a magic ring.
Rnd 1: 5 sc in ring—5 sc.
Rnd 2: Inc around—10 sc.
Rnd 3: [Sc, inc] around—15 sc.
Rnds 4–18: Sc around.
Fasten off.

Using photo as a guide, wrap Fhdc strap around doll and sew ends together and to top of Sheath.

Sword Handle

With **G** make a magic ring.
Rnd 1: 6 sc in ring—6 sc.
Rnd 2: Inc around—12 sc.
Rnds 3–4: Sc around.
Fasten off.
Fhdc 6 and fasten off leaving a long tail. Sew to side of Handle.

Sword Blade

With **E**, Fhdc 16 and fasten off leaving a long tail. Sew to Handle.
Weave in ends.

"I have given me word not to lay a finger or a hook on Peter Pan. And Captain Hook never breaks a promise."
—Captain Hook, *Peter Pan* (1953)

Cruella De Vil

Designed by Elise Speed

Skill Level: Easy

It's London, England, in the 1960s, and Cruella De Vil is in the market for a new, luxurious fur coat . . . Fortunately, no puppies were harmed in this animated film! Because entry into the pantheon of villainy starts with intentions, Cruella De Vil lands herself a spot even though her evil deeds were thankfully never achieved. If fashion is about self-expression, well, Cruella's taste sure says a lot. On a cold winter night, Ms. De Vil sends her two henchmen Horace and Jasper to the home of Roger and Anita Radcliffe when she discovers that their beautiful Dalmatians, Pongo and Perdita, have had a litter of fifteen Dalmatian puppies. This is just one stop on Cruella's heinous mission to puppy-nap across the city. However, Pongo and Perdita enlist the help of their fellow dogs to rescue all of London's missing puppies.

Cruella De Vil has one thing on her mind, and it's fashion. With her sleek black dress, her cute little shoes, and voluptuous coat, this crochet Cruella is styled to perfection for a night on the town. Her coat can be added or removed at any time, because she's known to stop at nothing for a change of wardrobe . . .

Cruella De Vil: **"Anita, darling!"**

Anita: **"How are you?"**

Cruella De Vil: **"Miserable, darling, as usual. Perfectly wretched!"**

—Conversation between Anita Radcliffe and Cruella De Vil, *One Hundred and One Dalmatians* (1961)

YARN

Worsted weight (#4 medium) yarn, shown in Lion Brand Basic Stitch Anti Pilling™ (100% acrylic, 185 yd. / 170 m per 3.5 oz. / 100 g skein)

Color A: #121L Almond, 1 skein

Color B: #153 Black, 1 skein

Color C: #400G Red Heather, 1 skein

Color D: #158L Mustard, 1 skein

Color E: #100 White, 1 skein

HOOK

US D (3.25 mm) crochet hook

NOTIONS

Pair of 10 mm safety eyes

Black embroidery floss

White embroidery floss

Pink blush (optional)

Stitch markers

Polyester stuffing

Yarn needle

Scissors

FINISHED MEASUREMENTS

Height: 12" / 30 cm

Width 3" / 7.5 cm

GAUGE

24 sc and 20 rnds = 4 in. / 10 cm in sc

Gauge is not critical for this project. Ensure your stitches are tight so the stuffing won't show through.

SPECIAL STITCHES

Inc (increase) = Work 2 sc in the next st

Invdec (invisible single crochet decrease) = Insert hook in front loop only of each of next 2 sts, yo and draw through both sts, yo and draw through 2 loops on hook—1 st decreased.

Sc3tog (single crochet 3 stitches together) = [Insert hook into next st, yo and draw up a loop] 3 times, yo and draw through all loops on hook—2 sts decreased.

Bobble (bobble stitch) = [Yo, insert hook into st, yo and draw up a loop, yo and draw through 2 loops on hook] 3 times, yo and draw through all loops on hook.

NOTES

- Work in continuous rounds unless otherwise indicated.
- When indicated, join at the end of a round with a slip stitch in the first stitch. To join new yarn to a stitch, insert hook in stitch and pull up a loop in indicated color.
- To change colors, work the last yarn over of the previous stitch with the new color. Fasten off previous color unless otherwise indicated.
- If desired, instead of making a magic ring, chain 2 and work indicated stitches in the 2nd chain from the hook.

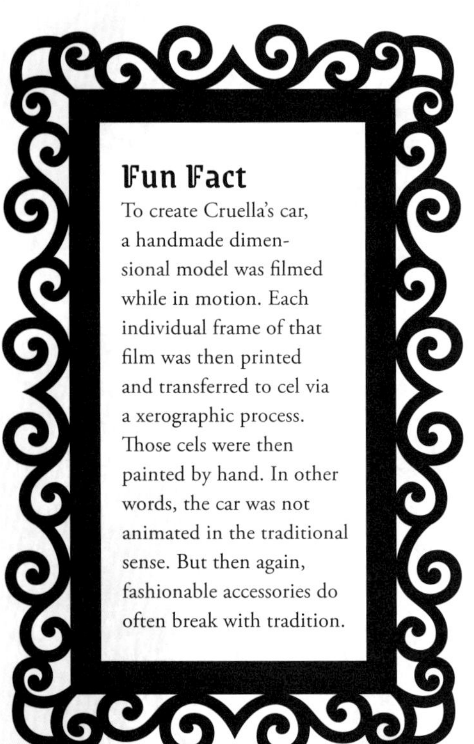

Fun Fact

To create Cruella's car, a handmade dimensional model was filmed while in motion. Each individual frame of that film was then printed and transferred to cel via a xerographic process. Those cels were then painted by hand. In other words, the car was not animated in the traditional sense. But then again, fashionable accessories do often break with tradition.

Legs (Make 2)

With **C**.

Rnd 1: Ch 5, starting in 2nd ch from hook, sc 3, 3 sc in last st, rotate to work on underside of starting ch, sc 2, inc—10 sc.

Rnd 2: Inc, sc 2, inc, sc, inc, sc 2, inc 2—15 sc.

Rnd 3: Inc, sc 4, inc, sc 2, inc, sc 4, inc 2—20 sc.

Rnd 4: Inc 2, sc 5, inc, sc 2, inc, sc 6, inc, sc 2—25 sc.

Rnd 5: Working in BLO, sc around.

Rnd 6: Sc 11, inc, sc 2, inc, sc 10—27 sc.

Rnd 7: Sc 11, [invdec] 4 times, sc 8—23 sc.

Rnd 8: Sc 10, [invdec] 3 times, sc 7—20 sc.

Change to **A**.

Rnd 9: Sc 9, [invdec] twice, sc 7—18 sc.

Rnd 10: Sc 9, sc3tog, sc 6—16 sc.

Rnds 11–30: Sc around.

Fasten off first Leg. Do not fasten off 2nd Leg. Continue to Body.

Body

Using st markers, mark center sc on inner side of each Leg.

Rnd 31: Sc around 2nd Leg to marked st, sc in marked st on 2nd Leg, sc in marked st on first Leg, sc around first Leg, sc in remaining sc on 2nd Leg—32 sc.

Rnd 32: [Sc 7, inc] 4 times—36 sc.

Rnd 33: [Sc 5, inc] around—42 sc.

Rnd 34: [Sc 6, inc] around—48 sc.

Rnds 35–38: Sc around.

Rnd 39: [Sc 6, invdec] around—42 sc.

Rnd 40: [Sc 5, invdec] around—36 sc.

Rnd 41: [Sc 4, invdec] around—30 sc.

Rnd 42: [Sc 3, invdec] around—24 sc.

Rnd 43: [Sc 3, inc] around—30 sc.

Rnd 44: [Sc 4, inc] around—36 sc.

Rnd 45: [Sc 5, inc] around—42 sc.

Rnd 46: [Sc 6, inc] around—48 sc.

Rnds 47–49: Sc around.

Rnd 50: [Sc 6, invdec] around—42 sc.

Rnd 51: [Sc 5, invdec] around—36 sc.

Rnd 52: [Sc 4, invdec] around—30 sc.

Rnd 53: [Sc 3, invdec] around—24 sc.

Rnd 54: Sc around.

Rnd 55: [Sc 2, invdec] around—18 sc.

Rnds 56–57: Sc around.

Rnd 58: [Sc 2, inc] around—24 sc.

Rnd 59: [Sc 3, inc] around—30 sc.

Rnd 60: [Sc 4, inc] around—36 sc.

Rnd 61: [Sc 5, inc] around—42 sc.

Rnd 62: [Sc 6, inc] around—48 sc.

Rnd 63: [Sc 7, inc] around—54 sc.

Rnd 64: [Sc 8, inc] around—60 sc.

Rnds 65–76: Sc around.

Rnd 77: [Sc 8, invdec] around—54 sc.

Add safety eyes at Rnd 70, 9 sts apart. Embroider eyebrows and eye details using black embroidery thread. With **A**, embroider nose at Rnd 68, 4 sts across.

Rnd 78: [Sc 7, invdec] around—48 sc.

Rnd 79: [Sc 6, invdec] around—42 sc.

Rnd 80: [Sc 5, invdec] around—36 sc.

Rnd 81: [Sc 4, invdec] around—30 sc.

Rnd 82: [Sc 3, invdec] around—24 sc.

Rnd 83: [Sc 2, invdec] around—18 sc.

Rnd 84: [Sc, invdec] around—12 sc.

Rnd 85: Invdec around—6 sc.

Make sure the Head is well stuffed before closing. Fasten off leaving a long tail. Sew remaining 6 sts closed in FLO. Weave in ends.

Arms (Make 2)

With **C** make a magic ring.
Rnd 1: 6 sc in ring—6 sc.
Rnd 2: Inc around—12 sc.
Rnd 3: Sc around.
Rnd 4: Sc, bobble, sc 10.
Rnds 5–13: Sc around.
Change to **A**.
Rnd 14: Working in BLO, sc around.
Rnds 15–21: Sc around.
Rnd 22: [Sc 2, invdec] 3 times—9 sc.
Fasten off, leaving a long tail. Sew Arms closed and sew to Rnd 54 of Body.

Dress

With **B**, leaving a long tail.
Row 1: Ch 37, starting in 2nd ch from hook, sc across, turn—36 sc.
Row 2: Ch 1, [sc 5, inc] around, turn—42 sc.
Row 3: Ch 1, [sc 6, inc] across, turn—48 sc.
Row 4: Ch 1, [sc 6, invdec] across, turn—42 sc.
Row 5: Ch 1, sc across, turn.
Row 6: Ch 1, [sc 5, invdec] across, turn—36 sc.
Row 7: Ch 1, sc across, turn.
Row 8: Ch 1, [sc 4, invdec] across, turn—30 sc.
Row 9: Ch 1, sc across, turn.
Row 10: Ch 1, [sc 4, inc] across, turn—36 sc.

Row 11: Ch 1, [sc 5, inc] across, turn—42 sc.
Row 12: Ch 1, [sc 6, inc] across, turn—48 sc.
Row 13: Ch 1, [sc 7, inc] across, turn—54 sc.
Row 14: Ch 1, sc across, do not turn, sc in first st of row to join.
Begin working in rnds.
Rnd 15: Sc around.
Rnd 16: [7 sc, invdec] around—48 sc.
Rnd 17: Sc around.
Rnd 18: [Sc 6, invdec] around—42 sc.
Rnds 19–27: Sc around.
Rnd 28: Working in BLO, sl st, ch 3 (*counts as dc here and throughout*), dc in same st, 2 dc in each st around, join—84 sc.
Rnd 29: Ch 3, dc around.
Fasten off.

Dress Straps (Make 2)

With **B**, leaving a long tail.
Row 1: Ch 14, starting in 2nd ch from hook, sc across, turn—13 sc.
Row 2: Sc across.
Fasten off leaving a long tail to sew.

Sew one end of each Strap to center front and other ends to the back edge of each side of the Dress. Sew back of Dress closed with a mattress seam.

Coat

With **D**.
Row 1: Ch 38**,** starting in 4th ch from hook (skipped chs count as dc) dc across, turn—36 dc.
Rows 2–3: Ch 3, dc in across, turn.
Row 4: Ch 3, working in BLO, dc across, turn.
Row 5: Ch 3, dc 5, ch 6, skip 6 (armhole made), dc 12, ch 6, skip 6 (armhole made), dc 6, turn—24 dc, 2 ch-6 sps.
Row 6: Ch 3, dc in each dc and ch across, turn—36 dc.
Row 7: Ch 3, dc 4, 2 dc in next st, [dc 5, 2 dc in next st] 4 times, dc 6, turn—41 dc.
Row 8: Ch 3, dc 5, 2 dc in next st, [dc 6, 2 dc in next st] 4 times, dc 6, turn—46 dc.
Row 9: Ch 3, dc 5, 2 dc in next st, [dc 7, 2 dc in next st] 3 times, dc 8, 2 dc in next st, dc 6, turn—51 dc.
Rows 10–16: Ch 3, dc across, turn.
Fasten off. Weave in ends.

Sleeves (Make 2)

With **D**, join in any skipped st on underside of the armhole.
Rnd 1: Ch 3, work 15 dc evenly around armhole, join—16 dc.
Rnd 2: Ch 3, dc around, join.

Rnd 3: Ch 3, dc 2, 2 dc in next st, [dc 3, 2 dc in next st] 3 times, join—20 sc.
Rnds 4–5: Ch 3, dc around, join.
Fasten off. Weave in ends.

Coat Border

With **D**, join yarn in bottom right corner of Coat, ch 1, sc in same corner, sc 25 evenly up coat opening, sc 4 evenly up collar, 3 sc in corner, sc 35 across top of coat, 3 sc in corner, sc 4 evenly down collar, sc 25 evenly down coat opening, 3 sc in corner at bottom edge, sc 50 across coat bottom, 2 sc in same corner as beginning join. Fasten off. Weave in ends.

Hair (Make 1 with B and 1 with E)

Make a magic ring.
Row 1: 6 sc in ring, turn—6 sc.
Row 2: Ch 1, [sc, inc] 3 times, turn—9 sc.
Row 3: Ch 1, [sc 2, inc] 3 times, turn—12 sc.
Row 4: Ch 1, [sc 3, inc] 3 times, turn—15 sc.
Row 5: Ch 1, [sc 4, inc] 3 times, turn—18 sc.
Row 6: Ch 1, [sc 5, inc] 3 times, turn—21 sc.
Begin working Hair Strands.
Strand 1: Ch 25, starting in 3rd ch from hook, 2 hdc in first ch, [3 hdc in next ch] 9 times, hdc 13, sl st in next st on Row 6.
Strand 2: Ch 25, starting in 3rd ch from hook, 2 hdc in first ch, [3 hdc in next ch] 9 times, hdc 13, sl st 2 on Row 6.
Strands 3–10: [Repeat strands 1 and 2] 3 times.
Strand 11: Repeat strand 1.
Strand 12: Ch 10, starting in 3rd ch from hook, hdc across, sl st in next st on Row 6.
Strand 13: Ch 5, starting in 3rd ch from hook, hdc across, sl st in next st on Row 6.
Strands 14–17: [Repeat strands 12 and 13] twice. Sl st in last st on Row 6.
Fasten off, leaving a long tail for seaming.
With **B** and **E**, sides together and short strands to front, use magic ring tails to join together with the mattress stitch. Sew Hair onto Head.

Finishing (Optional)

If you want to make Cruella De Vil look extra angry, add a bit of blush to both cheeks!

Gaston

Designed by Zac Doar

Skill Level: Easy

Dismissed! Rejected! Publicly humiliated! Why, it's more than the handsome and talented hunter Gaston can bear. There is no one in the little provincial town where Gaston lives who is more admired than him; he's everyone's favorite guy! But does that matter to the admittedly beautiful Belle, daughter of Maurice, the town tinkerer? No! Despite Gaston's best efforts, Belle won't give him the time of day, even when Gaston graciously tells her that she could be his wife . . . if she would just get her nose out of those books. She's infuriating! Belle seems to be avoiding Gaston at every opportunity, even going so far as to disappear for a time, only to suddenly reappear in the town with feelings for the dreadful Beast living in the enchanted castle in the forest! Well, that just won't do. Gaston will put a stop to Belle's misplaced affection, even if it means taking down the monster in the castle himself. If he can't have Belle, no one can.

With this pattern, you're so lucky! You get the chance to crochet your very own Gaston. After all, he's perfect, a true paragon. No one is as burly and brawny, and as you can see, he has biceps to spare! This crochet version of Gaston captures all of his handsome features but, our apologies, he may be lacking in the self-awareness department. He is a villain after all.

Gaston: **"How can you read this? There's no pictures!"**

Belle: **"Well, some people use their imagination."**

—Exchange between Gaston and Belle, *Beauty and the Beast* (1991)

YARN

Worsted weight (#4 medium) yarn, shown in Lion Brand Basic Stitch Anti Pilling™ (100% acrylic, 185 yd. / 170 m per 3.5 oz. / 100 g skein)

Color A: #408F Russet Heather, 1 skein
Color B: #153 Black, 1 skein
Color C: #400G Red Heather, 1 skein
Color D: #158L Mustard, 1 skein
Color E: #121L Almond, 1 skein

HOOK

US D (3.25 mm) crochet hook

NOTIONS

Pair of 15 mm black safety eyes
Stitch markers
Polyester stuffing
Yarn needle
Scissors

FINISHED MEASUREMENTS

Height: 9" / 22.5 cm
Width: 4"/ 10 cm

GAUGE

24 sc and 24 rnds = 4 in. / 10 cm in sc

Gauge is not critical for this project. Ensure your stitches are tight so the stuffing won't show through.

SPECIAL STITCHES

Inc (increase) = Work 2 sc in the next st.

Invdec (invisible single crochet decrease) = Insert hook in front loop only of each of next 2 sts, yo and draw through both sts, yo and draw through 2 loops on hook—1 st decreased.

Bobble (bobble stitch) = [Yo, insert hook into st, yo and draw up a loop, yo and draw through 2 loops on hook] 5 times, yo and draw through all loops on hook.

Gaston

Designed by Zac Doar

Skill Level: Easy

Dismissed! Rejected! Publicly humiliated! Why, it's more than the handsome and talented hunter Gaston can bear. There is no one in the little provincial town where Gaston lives who is more admired than him; he's everyone's favorite guy! But does that matter to the admittedly beautiful Belle, daughter of Maurice, the town tinkerer? No! Despite Gaston's best efforts, Belle won't give him the time of day, even when Gaston graciously tells her that she could be his wife . . . if she would just get her nose out of those books. She's infuriating! Belle seems to be avoiding Gaston at every opportunity, even going so far as to disappear for a time, only to suddenly reappear in the town with feelings for the dreadful Beast living in the enchanted castle in the forest! Well, that just won't do. Gaston will put a stop to Belle's misplaced affection, even if it means taking down the monster in the castle himself. If he can't have Belle, no one can.

With this pattern, you're so lucky! You get the chance to crochet your very own Gaston. After all, he's perfect, a true paragon. No one is as burly and brawny, and as you can see, he has biceps to spare! This crochet version of Gaston captures all of his handsome features but, our apologies, he may be lacking in the self-awareness department. He is a villain after all.

Gaston: "How can you read this? There's no pictures!"

Belle: "Well, some people use their imagination."

—Exchange between Gaston and Belle, *Beauty and the Beast* (1991)

YARN

Worsted weight (#4 medium) yarn, shown in Lion Brand Basic Stitch Anti Pilling™ (100% acrylic, 185 yd. / 170 m per 3.5 oz. / 100 g skein)

Color A: #408F Russet Heather, 1 skein
Color B: #153 Black, 1 skein
Color C: #400G Red Heather, 1 skein
Color D: #158L Mustard, 1 skein
Color E: #121L Almond, 1 skein

HOOK

US D (3.25 mm) crochet hook

NOTIONS

Pair of 15 mm black safety eyes
Stitch markers
Polyester stuffing
Yarn needle
Scissors

FINISHED MEASUREMENTS

Height: 9" / 22.5 cm
Width: 4"/ 10 cm

GAUGE

24 sc and 24 rnds = 4 in. / 10 cm in sc

Gauge is not critical for this project. Ensure your stitches are tight so the stuffing won't show through.

SPECIAL STITCHES

Inc (increase) = Work 2 sc in the next st.

Invdec (invisible single crochet decrease) = Insert hook in front loop only of each of next 2 sts, yo and draw through both sts, yo and draw through 2 loops on hook—1 st decreased.

Bobble (bobble stitch) = [Yo, insert hook into st, yo and draw up a loop, yo and draw through 2 loops on hook] 5 times, yo and draw through all loops on hook.

NOTES

- Work in continuous rounds unless otherwise indicated.
- When indicated, join at the end of a round with a slip stitch in the first stitch. To join new yarn to a stitch, insert hook in stitch and pull up a loop in indicated color.
- To change colors, work the last yarn over of the previous stitch with the new color. Fasten off previous color unless otherwise indicated.
- If desired, instead of making a magic ring, chain 2 and work indicated stitches in the 2nd chain from the hook.
- Gaston's clothes are crocheted as part of the body, not as separate pieces.

Fun Fact

At the end of his fight with the Beast, when Gaston falls, the pupils of his eyes are replaced by skulls for two frames.

Boots (Make 2)

With **A**.

Rnd 1: Ch 7, starting in 2nd ch from hook, 5 sc, inc, rotate to work in underside of starting ch, 5 sc, inc in skipped ch—14 sc.

Rnd 2: [Sc, inc] around—21 sc.

Rnd 3: Sc 7, [inc, sc] twice, inc, sc 9—24 sc.

Rnd 4: Working in BLO, sc around.

Rnds 5–6: Sc around.

Rnd 7: Sc 7, [invdec] 6 times, sc 5—18 sc.

Rnd 8: Sc 5, [invdec] 4 times, sc 5—14 sc.

Rnds 9–11: Sc around.

Rnd 12: Working in FLO, [sc, inc] around—21 sc.

Rnd 13–15: Sc around.

Fasten off. Weave in ends.

Legs (Make 2)

With **B**, join to first unworked BL of Rnd 11 on Boot.

Rnd 1: Working in unworked BLO**,** sc around—14 sc.

Rnds 2–7: Sc around.

Fasten off first Leg. Do not fasten off 2nd Leg. Continue to Body.

Body

Rnd 1: Sc 7 on 2nd Leg, ch 2, sc around first Leg, inc in 2 chs, sc in remaining sts on 2nd Leg—32 sc.

Rnds 2–5: Sc around.

Change to **C**.

Rnd 6: Sc around.

Stuff the Body and Legs and continue stuffing as you work.

Rnd 7: Working in BLO, sc around.

Rnds 8–11: Sc around.

Rnd 12: Sc 2, inc, sc 15, inc, sc 13—34 sc.

Rnds 13–15: Sc around.

Rnd 16: Sc 2, inc, sc 16, inc, sc 14—36 sc.

Rnds 17–19: Sc around.

Rnd 20: [Sc, invdec] around—24 sc.

Rnd 21: [Sc, invdec] around—16 sc.

Change to **E**.

Rnd 22: Working in BLO, sc around.

Rnd 23: Invdec around—8 sc.

Rnd 24: Inc around—16 sc.

Rnd 25: [Sc, inc] around—24 sc.

Rnd 26: [Sc, inc, sc] around—32 sc.

Rnd 27: [Sc 3, inc] around—40 sc.

Rnd 28: [Sc 2, inc, sc 2] around—48 sc.

Rnds 29–39: Sc around.

Add 15 mm safety eyes between Rnds 34 and 35. Make sure the centers of the eyes line up with the center of the Boots and leave about 7 visible stitches between the eyes.

Rnd 40: [Sc 2, invdec, sc 2] around—40 sc.

Rnd 41: [Sc 3, invdec] around—32 sc.

Rnd 42: [Sc, invdec, sc] around—24 sc.

Rnd 43: [Sc, invdec] around—16 sc.

Rnd 44: Invdec around—8 sc.

Fasten off, leaving a long tail. Sew remaining 8 sts closed through FLO. Weave in ends.

Base of Shirt

With Body upside down, join **C** to last unworked FL of Rnd 6 on Body.
Rnd 1: Working in unworked FLO, [sc 7, inc] around—36 sc.
Rnd 2: Sc around.
Fasten off. Weave in ends.

Collar

With **D**.
Row 1: Ch 19, starting in 3rd ch from hook, 2 dc in first ch, hdc 2, sc 11, hdc 2, 3 dc in last ch.
Fasten off, leaving a long tail. Use tail to sew Collar to the base of neck, leaving a small gap at front center.

First Arm

With **D** make a magic ring.
Rnd 1: 6 sc in ring—6 sc.
Rnd 2: Inc around—12 sc.
Rnd 3: [Sc 2, inc] around—16 sc.
Rnds 4–5: Sc around.
Rnd 6: Bobble, 15 sc.
Rnd 7: Sc around.
Rnd 8: [Sc 2, invdec] around—12 sc.
Rnd 9: Sc around.
Rnd 10: Working in FLO, [sc, inc] around—18 sc.
Rnd 11: Sc around.
Fasten off.
With **E**, join yarn to the first unworked BL of Rnd 9.
Rnd 12: Working in unworked BLO, sc around—12 sc.
Begin stuffing Arm and continue stuffing as you go.
Rnds 13–18: Sc around.
Change to **C**.
Rnd 19: Working in BLO, sl st around.
Rnd 20: Working in BLO, sc around.
Rnds 21–23: Sc around.
Rnd 24: Invdec around—6 sc.
Fasten off, leaving a long tail. Sew remaining 6 sts closed through FLO. Sew to Body, with bobble facing toward front. Weave in ends.

Second Arm

With **D** make a magic ring.
Rnds 1–5: Repeat Rnds 1–5 of First Arm.
Rnd 6: 8 sc, bobble, 7 sc.
Complete as for First Arm.

Belt

With **B**.
Row 1: Ch 39, starting in 2nd ch from hook, sc across—38 sc.
Fasten off leaving a long tail for sewing. Sew both short ends of the Belt together making sure not to twist. Attach the Belt to Body just above the base of the shirt.
Using **D**, embroider a small square onto the front of the Belt.

Finishing

Cut approximately 60 pieces of **B** measuring 10" long. Use your hook to pull a strand through each stitch on top of Gaston's Head, forming a new loop on your hook. Yarn over and use your hook to pull both the loose ends through the loop on your hook. Then, tighten the loop down.
You will only need to add these pieces of yarn to the hairline. Once all the pieces of yarn have been attached, gather them over the back of the Head and tie together with a small piece of **C** In a low ponytail. Trim the ends.
Using **B**, embroider eyebrows just above each of the safety eyes. Using **E**, embroider a small nose just between the safety eyes.

Shere Khan

Designed by Lee Sartori

Skill Level: Easy

If there's one thing Shere Khan expects the creatures of *his* jungle to know, it's that *he's* the one they should fear. He may speak politely and evaluate his options before acting, but when he does act, he's ferocious. However, the mighty Shere Khan has his own fears: fire, and the humans who make it. So, when a young human, Mowgli, shows up in his jungle, Shere Khan is less than welcoming. And when the boy has the gall to show no fear standing before Shere Khan, Mowgli's presence becomes unacceptable. Besides, where one human goes, more tend to follow. And if there's something Shere Khan won't risk, it's allowing humans in his jungle. Mowgli may have escaped him the first time, but Shere Khan isn't planning to let that happen again.

Shere Khan may be a fearsome tiger in *The Jungle Book*, but in amigurumi form, he looks more like a friendly feline than a frightening predator. (We think.) Still, it couldn't hurt to keep an eye on him.

"You should also know that everyone runs from Shere Khan."

—Shere Khan, *The Jungle Book* (1967)

YARN

Worsted weight (#4 medium) yarn, shown in WeCrochet Swish (100% fine superwash merino wool, 110 yd. / 100 m per 1.75 oz. / 50 g ball)

Color A: White, 1 ball
Color B: California Poppy, 2 balls
Color C: Phoenix, 1 ball
Color D: Dijon, 1 ball
Color E: Black, 1 ball

HOOK

US D (3.25 mm) crochet hook

NOTIONS

Stitch markers
Polyester stuffing
Yarn needle
Scissors

FINISHED MEASUREMENTS

Height: 8" / 20 cm
Width: 7" / 17.5 cm

SPECIAL STITCHES

Inc (increase) = Work 2 sc in the next st.

Invdec (invisible single crochet decrease) = Insert hook in front loop only of each of next 2 sts, yo and draw through both sts, yo and draw through 2 loops on hook—1 st decreased.

GAUGE

28 sc and 28 rnds = 4 in. / 10 cm in sc

Gauge is not critical for this project. Ensure your stitches are tight so the stuffing won't show through.

NOTES

- Work in continuous rounds unless otherwise indicated.
- When indicated, join at the end of a round with a slip stitch in the first stitch. To join new yarn to a stitch, insert hook in stitch and pull up a loop in indicated color.
- To change colors, work the last yarn over of the previous stitch with the new color. Fasten off previous color unless otherwise indicated.
- If desired, instead of making a magic ring, chain 2 and work indicated stitches in the 2nd chain from the hook.

Single Toes (Make 12)

With **A** make a magic ring.

Rnd 1: 6 sc in ring—6 sc.

Rnd 2: Sc around.

Fasten off.

Feet (Make 4)

Make a Single Toe, but do not fasten off.

Next rnd will join current Toe with 3 additional Single Toes together.

Rnd 1: Sc 3 on current Toe, sc 3 on each of next 2 Toes, sc 6 around last Toe, sc 3 on backside of each of 2 center Toes, sc 3 on current Toe—24 sc.

Rnd 2: Sc around.

Change to **B**.

Rnd 3: Ch 1, working in BLO sc around, join.

Rnd 4: Ch 1, [sc 3, invdec, sc 3] around, join—21 sc.

Rnds 5–7: Sc around.

Rnd 8: Ch 1, sc 2, ch 7, skip next 7 sts (*leg opening made*), sc 12, join—14 sc, 7 chs.

Rnd 9: Ch 1, sc in each ch and st around, join—21 sc.

Rnd 10: Ch 1, [invdec, sc 5] around, join—18 sc.

Rnd 11: Ch 1, [invdec, sc] around, join—12 sc.

Rnd 12: Ch 1, invdec around, join—6 sc.

Fasten off, leaving a long tail for sewing. Sew remaining 6 sts closed. Weave in end. Stuff Foot.

Back Legs (Make 2)

With **B**, join to first skipped sc of Rnd 7 of Foot.

Rnd 1: Ch 1, sc 7 in skipped sc, sc in gap before underside of ch-7, sc in underside of next 7 chs, sc in gap before first sc, join—16 sc.

Rnd 2: Ch 1 tightly, [inc, sc 7] around, do not join—18 sc.

Rnds 3–7: Sc around.

Rnd 8: [Sc, inc, sc] around—24 sc.

Rnd 9: Sc around.

Rnd 10: [Sc, invdec, sc] around—18 sc.

Rnd 11: [Invdec, sc] around—12 sc.

Stuff.

Rnd 12: Invdec around—6 sc.

Fasten off, leaving a long tail for sewing. Sew remaining 6 sts closed.

Back Leg Inner Pads (Make 2)

With **A**.

Rnd 1: Ch 9, starting in 2nd ch from hook, sc 7, 3 sc in last ch, rotate to work in underside of ch, sc 7, 3 sc in skipped ch, join—20 sc.

Fasten off, leaving a long tail for sewing. Sew Inner Pad to inside edge of each Leg. Weave in ends.

Front Legs (Make 2)

With **B** join to first skipped st of Rnd 7 of Foot.

Rnd 1: Ch 1, sc 7, sc in gap before underside of ch-7, sc in underside of next 7 chs, sc in gap before first sc, join—16 sc.

Rnds 2–12: Sc around. Fasten off. Stuff Leg. Set aside to join to Body.

Body

With **B** make a magic ring.

Rnd 1: 6 sc in ring—6 sc.

Rnd 2: Inc around—12 sc.

Rnd 3: [Inc, sc] around—18 sc.

Rnd 4: [Sc, inc, sc] around—24 sc.

Rnd 5: [Inc, sc 3] around—30 sc.

Rnd 6: [Sc 2, inc, sc 2] around—36 sc.

Rnd 7: [Inc, sc 5] around—42 sc.

Rnd 8: [Sc 3, inc, sc 3] around—48 sc.

Rnd 9: [Inc, sc 7] around—54 sc.

Rnds 10–24: Sc around.

Rnd 25: [Invdec, sc 7] around—48 sc.

Hold Front Legs in line with Body to join in next Rnd.

Rnd 26: Sc 3, sc in back of first Front Leg, sc in next 15 sts of Front Leg, sc 9 on Body, sc in back of 2nd Front Leg, sc in next 15 sts of 2nd Front Leg, sc 36 on Body—80 sc.
Rnd 27: Sc around.
Rnd 28: [Sc 4, invdec, sc 4] around—72 sc.
Rnd 29: Sc around.
Rnd 30: [Sc 5, invdec, sc 5] around—66 sc.
Rnd 31: Sc around.
Rnd 32: [Invdec, sc 9] around—60 sc.
Rnd 33: Sc around.
Rnd 34: [Sc 4, invdec, sc 4] around—54 sc.
Rnd 35: Sc around.
Rnd 36: [Invdec, sc 7] around—48 sc.
Rnds 37–39: Sc around.
Rnd 40: [Sc 3, invdec, sc 3] around—42 sc.
Rnd 41: Sc around.
Rnd 42: [Invdec, sc 5] around—36 sc.
Rnd 43: Sc around.
Rnd 44: [Sc 2, invdec, sc 2] around—30 sc.
Rnd 45: Sc around.
Sew Back Legs to either side of Body. Continue to Head.

Head

With **B**.
Rnd 1: Inc around—60 sc.
Rnds 2–9: Sc around.
Rnd 10: [Sc 9, invdec, sc 9] around—57 sc.
Rnd 11: [Invdec, sc 17] around—54 sc.
Rnd 12: [Sc 8, invdec, sc 8] around—51 sc.
Rnd 13: [Invdec, sc 15] around—48 sc.
Rnd 14: [Sc 3, invdec, sc 3] around—42 sc.
Rnd 15: [Invdec, sc 5] around—36 sc.
Rnd 16: [Sc 2, invdec, sc 2] around—30 sc.
Stuff Head. Continue stuffing as work progresses.
Rnd 17: [Invdec, sc 3] around—24 sc.
Rnd 18: [Sc, invdec, sc] around—18 sc.
Rnd 19: [Invdec, sc] around—12 sc.
Rnd 20: Invdec around—6 sc.
Fasten off, leaving a long tail for sewing. Sew remaining 6 sts closed. Weave in end.

Lower Jaw

With **A**.
Rnd 1: Ch 5, starting in 2nd ch from hook, sc 3, 3 sc in last ch, rotate to work in underside of ch, sc 3, 3 sc in skipped ch—12 sc.
Rnd 2: [Sc 3, inc 3] around—18 sc.
Rnd 3: *Sc 3, [inc, sc] 3 times; repeat from * around—24 sc.
Rnds 4–6: Sc around.
Fasten off, leaving a long tail for sewing. Stuff piece. Sew Lower Jaw to Head between Rnds 1 and 5. Weave in ends.

Muzzle

With **A** make a magic ring.
Rnd 1: 6 sc in ring—6 sc.
Rnd 2: Inc around—12 sc.
Rnd 3: [Inc, sc] around—18 sc.
Rnd 4: Sc around.
Begin working in rows.
Rnd 5: Sc 6, hdc 3, [2 dc in next st] 6 times, hdc 3, turn—24 sts.
Row 6: Ch 1, hdc 3, dc 12, hdc 3, leave remaining sts unworked—18 sts.
Fasten off, leaving a long tail for sewing. Stuff piece. Sew Muzzle directly above Lower Jaw, between Rnds 5 and 12.

Nose

With **B**.
Row 1: Ch 5, starting in 2nd ch from hook, sc 4, turn—4 sc.
Row 2: Ch 1, inc, sc 2, inc, turn—6 sc.
Rows 3–6: Ch 1, sc across, turn.
Fasten off, leaving a long tail for sewing. Sew Nose on top of Muzzle with the last row of the Nose touching Rnd 12.

Nose Tip

With **C**.
Row 1: Ch 2, 3 sc in 2nd ch from hook, turn—3 sc.
Row 2: (Ch 2, dc, ch 2) in first st, (sc, ch 2) in next st, 2 dc in last—4 sts.
Fasten off, leaving a long tail for sewing. Sew Nose Tip to bottom of Nose. Weave in ends.

Ears (Make 2)

With **B** make a magic ring.
Rnd 1: 6 sc in ring—6 sc.
Rnd 2: Inc around—12 sc.

Fasten off, leaving a long tail for sewing. Sew Ears to sides of Head in line with top of Nose. Weave in ends.

Eyes (Make 2)

With **D** make a magic ring.

Rnd 1: 6 sc in ring, join—6 sc.

Change to **A**.

Rnd 2: Ch 1, inc, 2 hdc in next st, [2 dc in next st] twice, 2 hdc in next st, inc, join—12 sts.

Fasten off, leaving a long tail for sewing. Using a length of **E**, embroider a small line to inside of Eye using photo as a guide. Sew Eye to Head between Rnds 9 and 15. Weave in ends. Using a length of **E** held double, add eyebrows above Eyes.

Belly Patch

With **A**.

Row 1: Ch 7, starting in 2nd ch from hook, sc across, turn—6 sc.

Rows 2–27: Ch 1, sc across, turn.

Row 28: *Ch 7, starting in 2nd ch from hook, sc, hdc 2, dc 3; skip 2 sts on Row 27**, sl st, repeat from * to **, sl st in last st, rotate to work along row ends, sc 27 across row ends, sc 6 across underside of starting ch, sc 27 evenly across opposite edge row ends, join.

Fasten off, leaving a long tail for sewing. Sew Belly Patch to front of Body between Front Legs.

Weave in ends.

Tail

With **B** make a magic ring. Stuff shape very lightly as work progresses.

Rnd 1: 6 sc in ring—6 sc.

Rnds 2–32: Sc around.

Fasten off, leaving a long tail for sewing. Sew Tail to bottom back of Body.

Finishing

Using **A**, cut approximately 20 pieces of yarn 4" long. Loop pieces through fabric to secure from Muzzle to Ear on either side of Head. Trim yarn to about 1" long. Using **E**, add black stripes to Head, Body, Tail, and Legs using photos as a guide. Weave in ends.

Bellwether

Designed by Lee Sartori

Skill Level: Easy

The city of Zootopia is a mammal metropolis where everyone from the largest elephant to the smallest shrew live and thrive. Everything is perfectly splendid, unless, that is, you are a prey animal rather than a predator. Assistant Mayor Dawn Bellwether is tired of being a sheep in a city of wolves (and tigers, and lions, and lots of other scary things)! She hatches a plan to take over the mayoral office to ensure the predators will be put in their place and the prey animals will rule Zootopia. The plan would have gone off without a hitch if it weren't for the new police rabbit with a personal mission to prove herself, and a nose for trouble. If Judy Hopps would just stay out of Assistant Mayor Bellwether's business, things would go much more smoothly!

Assistant Mayor Bellwether is a sweet sheep with a little voice and a lot of wool, who constantly finds herself under the foot of the grandiloquent Mayor Lionheart. Or so it seems. Her smart suit and glasses may come off as "business as usual," but her evil plots are larger than life. It might be best not to discount this pattern—it may surprise you!

"We're on the same team, Judy. Underestimated, underappreciated. Aren't you sick of it? Predators. They may be strong and loud . . . but prey outnumber predators ten to one. Think of it. Ninety percent of the population . . . united against a common enemy. We'll be unstoppable."

—Dawn Bellwether, *Zootopia* (2016)

YARN

Worsted weight (#4 medium) yarn, shown in WeCrochet Swish (100% fine superwash merino wool, 110 yd. / 100 m per 1.75 oz. / 50 g ball)

Color A: Cider, 1 ball
Color B: Frosting, 1 ball
Color C: Nutmeg Heather, 1 ball
Color D: Black, 1 ball
Color E: Shortbread, 1 ball
Color F: Delft Heather, 1 ball

HOOK

US D (3.25 mm) crochet hook
US 2 (1.5 mm) steel crochet hook

NOTIONS

Black embroidery thread
Pair of 9 mm black safety eyes
White felt
Green felt
Stitch markers
Polyester stuffing
Yarn needle
Scissors

FINISHED MEASUREMENTS

Height: 10" / 25 cm
Width: 9" / 22.5 cm

SPECIAL STITCHES

Inc (increase) = Work 2 sc in next st.

Invdec (invisible single crochet decrease) = Insert hook in front loop only of each of next 2 sts, yo and draw through both sts, yo and draw through 2 loops on hook—1 st decreased.

Mexsc (modified extended single crochet) = Insert hook into indicated st, yo and draw up a loop, [yo and draw through 1 loop] twice, yo and draw through 2 loops. *Note: Make your next sc tightly to secure this stitch.

GAUGE

28 sc and 28 rnds = 4 in. / 10 cm in sc

Gauge is not critical for this project. Ensure your stitches are tight so the stuffing won't show through.

NOTES

- Work in continuous rounds unless otherwise indicated.
- When indicated, join at the end of a round with a slip stitch in the first stitch. To join new yarn to a stitch, insert hook in stitch and pull up a loop in indicated color.
- To change colors, work the last yarn over of the previous stitch with the new color. Fasten off previous color unless otherwise indicated.
- If desired, instead of making a magic ring, chain 2 and work indicated stitches in the 2nd chain from the hook.
- The only piece worked with a 1.5 mm hook is the glasses. Use larger hook for all other parts of the pattern.

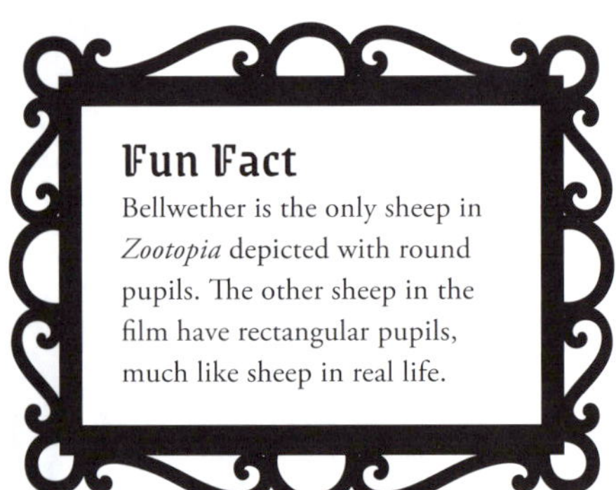

Fun Fact

Bellwether is the only sheep in *Zootopia* depicted with round pupils. The other sheep in the film have rectangular pupils, much like sheep in real life.

Toes (Make 8)

With **A**, make a magic ring.

Rnd 1: 3 sc in ring—3 sc.

Rnd 2: Inc, sc 2—4 sc.

Fasten off first Toe; do not fasten off 2nd Toe. Continue to join.

Rnd 3 (joining): Sc 2, sc around first Toe to join, sc in last 2 sts of 2nd Toe—8 sc.

Rnd 4: Sc around, join.

Fasten off. Set Toes aside to join for Foot and Arm.

Feet (Make 2)

With **B**, join to next st of Toe in BL.

Rnd 1: Ch 1, working in BLO sc around, join—8 sc.

Rnd 2: Ch 1, sc around, join.

Rnd 3: Ch 4, skip next 4 sts (*leg opening made*), sc in last 4 sts, join—4 sc, 4 chs.

Rnd 4: Ch 1, sc in each ch and st around, join—8 sc.

Rnd 5: Ch 1, invdec around, join—4 sc.

Fasten off, leaving a long tail for sewing. Sew remaining sts closed. Weave in end.

Legs (Make 2)

With **B**, join to first skipped st of Rnd 2 of Foot.

Rnd 1: Ch 1, sc 4, sc in gap before underside of ch 4, sc in underside of next 4 chs, sc in gap before first sc, join—10 sc.

Change to **C**.

Rnd 2: Ch 1 tightly, mexsc around, do not join.

Rnd 3: [Inc, sc 4] around—12 sc.

Rnd 4: Mexsc around.

Rnd 5: Sc around.

Rnd 6: Mexsc around.

Rnd 7: [Inc, sc] around—18 sc.

Rnd 8: Mexsc around.

Rnd 9: [Sc, inc, sc] around—24 sc.

Fasten off first Leg, do not fasten off 2nd Leg. Using st markers, mark center st at inner thigh of each Leg where Legs will meet.

Rnd 10: Sc around 2nd Leg to first marked st, sl st in marked st, sl st in marked st of first Leg to join, ch 1, exsc around each Leg—48 sts.

Rnd 11: [Inc, sc 7] around—54 sc.

Rnd 12: Mexsc around.

Rnd 13: Sc around.

Rnds 14–27: Repeat Rnds 12–13.
Rnd 28: [Invdec, sc 7] around—48 sc.
Rnd 29: [Mexsc 3, invdec, mexsc 3] around—42 sts.
Rnd 30: [Invdec, sc 5] around—36 sc.
Rnd 31: [Mexsc 2, invdec, mexsc 2] around—30 sts.
Rnd 32: [Invdec, sc 3] around—24 sc.
Rnd 33: Inc around—48 sc.
Rnd 34: [Inc, sc 7] around—54 sc.
Rnd 35: Mexsc around.
Rnd 36: Sc around.
Rnds 37–44: Repeat Rnds 35–36.
Rnd 45: Mexsc around.
Rnd 46: [Invdec, sc 7] around—48 sc.
Rnd 47: [Sc 3, invdec, sc 3] around—42 sc.
Rnd 48: Mexsc around.
Rnd 49: Sc around.
Rnds 50–51: Repeat Rnds 48–49.
Rnd 52: Repeat Rnd 48.
Rnd 53: [Invdec, sc 5] around—36 sc.
Stuff. Continue stuffing as work progresses.
Rnd 54: [Mexsc 2, invdec, mexsc 2] around—30 sts.
Rnd 55: [Invdec, sc 3] around—24 sc.
Rnd 56: [Mexsc, invdec, mexsc] around—18 sc.
Rnd 57: [Invdec, sc] around—12 sc.
Rnd 58: Invdec around—6 sc.
Fasten off, leaving a long tail for sewing. Sew remaining 6 sts closed. Weave in ends.

Face

With **B**, make a magic ring.
Rnd 1: 6 sc in ring—6 sc.
Rnd 2: [Inc, sc] around—9 sc.
Rnd 3: [Sc, inc, sc] around—12 sc.
Rnd 4: [Inc, sc] around—18 sc.
Begin working in turned rows.
Row 5: [Sc, inc, sc] 4 times, turn leaving remaining sts unworked—16 sc.
Row 6: Ch 1, [inc, sc 3] 4 times, turn—20 sc.
Row 7: Ch 1, [sc 3, hdc, dc 2, hdc, sc 3] twice, turn.
Row 8: Repeat Row 7.
Row 9: Repeat Row 7 do not turn.
Begin working in joined rounds.
Rnd 10: Ch 1, sc in each of 4 row ends, sc in unworked sts of Rnd 4,

sc in each of next 4 row ends, sc 20, join—34 sc.
Change to **C**.
Rnd 11: Ch 1, exsc around, join.
Fasten off, leaving a long tail for sewing. With green felt, add a ring around safety eye. Add another ring of white felt to back of green. Insert eyes to Face at Rnds 5–6 on either side of nose. Using a length of **D**, add eyelashes to sides of each eye. With **D** add eyebrows to Rnd 10 of Face above each eye. Stuff Face lightly and sew to front of Head between Rnds 35–46. Weave in ends.

Ears (Make 2)

With **B** make a magic ring.
Rnd 1: 6 sc in ring.
Rnd 2: Inc around—12 sc.
Rnd 3: [Inc, sc] around—18 sc.
Rnd 4: [Sc, inc, sc] around—24 sc.
Begin working in turned rows.
Row 5: Sc 9, turn leaving remaining sts unworked—9 sc.
Rows 6–7: Ch 1, sc across, turn.
Change to **C**.
Row 8: Ch 1, mexsc across, turn.
Row 9: Ch 1, mexsc across.
Fasten off, leaving a long tail for sewing. Sew Ears to either side of Head in line with top of Face. Pinch circle in **B** to shape.

Glasses

With **A** and 1.5 mm hook.
Row 1: Ch 56, starting in the 2nd ch from the hook, sc 15, ch 25, skip next 10 sts, sc 5, ch 25, skip next 10 sts, sc 15—35 sc, 2 ch-25 openings. Fasten off, leaving a long tail for sewing. Sew Glasses to front of Face.

Arms (Make 2)

With **B**, join to Toe in BL.
Rnd 1: Ch 1, in BLO sc around—8 sc.
Rnds 2–8: Sc around.
Change to **C**.
Rnd 9: [Inc, sc] around—12 sc.
Rnd 10: Mexsc around.
Rnd 11: Sc around.
Rnds 12–17: Repeat Rnds 10–11.
Fasten off, leaving a long tail for sewing. Stuff Arm Lightly. Sew to top of Body on either side.

Dress Panels (Make 2)

Starting with **D**, alternate between **D** and **E** after each row.
Row 1 (WS): Ch 31, starting in 2nd ch from hook, [sc, dc] across, turn—30 sts.
Rows 2–18: Ch 1, [sc, dc] across, turn.
Fasten off, leaving a long tail for sewing. Place 2 panels together with WS facing outward. Sew 8 sts on each shoulder closed leaving remaining sts open for Head. Sew seam from Row 1 to Row 14 on either side of dress. Weave in ends. Turn RS out. Add dress to Body.

Coat Back Panel

With **F**.
Row 1: Ch 31, starting in 2nd ch from hook sc across, turn—30 sc.
Rows 2–13: Ch 1, sc across, turn.
Fasten off. Skip first 5 sts, join to 6th st.
Row 14: Ch 1, sc 20, turn leaving remaining sts unworked—20 sc.
Rows 15–19: Ch 1, sc across, turn.
Fasten off, leaving a long tail for sewing.

Coat Front Left Panel

With **F**.
Row 1: Ch 16, starting in 2nd ch from hook sc across, turn—15 sc.
Rows 2–13: Ch 1, sc across, turn.
Row 14: Ch 1, sc 10, turn leaving remaining sts unworked—10 sc.
Rows 15–19: Ch 1, sc 10, turn.
Fasten off leaving a long tail for sewing.

Coat Front Right Panel

With **F**.
Rows 1–13: Repeat Rows 1–13 of Coat Front Left Panel.
Fasten off, skip first 5 sts, join to 6th st.
Row 14: Ch 1, sc 10, turn.
Rows 15–19: Ch 1, sc across, turn.
Fasten off leaving a long tail for sewing.

Sleeves (Make 2)

With **F**.

Row 1: Ch 13, starting in 2nd ch from hook sc across, turn—12 sc.

Rows 2–9: Ch 1, sc across, turn.

Fasten off leaving a long tail for sewing.

Coat Assembly

Place Front Left and Right Panels on Back Panel. Seam 5 sts of shoulder closed on each side leaving remaining 5 sts of Front Panels unseamed for collar. Insert Sleeves to side of each armhole and sew in place. Sew from wrist to underarm seam closed, and from underarm to hem closed on each side of Coat. Weave in ends.

Finishing

Add Coat to Body. Using a length of **F**, secure front of Coat closed by sewing it shut at bottom edge. Fold collar down on either side.

Oogie Boogie

Designed by Lee Sartori

Skill Level: Easy

Well, well, well, everyone in Halloween Town seems to be talking about Sandy Claws. At least, that's what that no-account Oogie Boogie aims to confirm. However, as he's been banished to an underground lair for previously trying to take over the town, any news takes a while to reach him. He'll get the mischievous trio Lock, Shock, and Barrel to kidnap Mister Sandy Claws so he can see what all the fuss is about and show Jack Skellington, the so-called Pumpkin King, who's *really* the King of Halloween Town. Oogie Boogie's the meanest guy around—just make sure he doesn't split a seam.

One piece of information we can confirm: This crocheted version of Oogie Boogie is decidedly not filled with bugs. Still, we wouldn't recommend opening him up to check—even in crochet form, we should all be very, very afraid.

"J-J-JACK! But they said you were dead. You must be double dead!"

—Oogie Boogie, *Tim Burton's The Nightmare Before Christmas* (1993)

YARN
Worsted weight (#4 medium) yarn, shown in WeCrochet Swish (100% fine superwash merino wool, 110 yd. / 100 m per 1.75 oz. / 50 g ball)
Color A: Granny Smith, 2 balls
Color B: Black, 1 ball

HOOK
US D (3.25 mm) crochet hook

NOTIONS
Black embroidery thread
10" Styrofoam ball
Black felt
Glue
Stitch markers
Polyester stuffing
Yarn needle
Scissors

FINISHED MEASUREMENTS
Height: 9" / 22.5 cm
Width: 5" / 12.5 cm

SPECIAL STITCHES
Inc (increase) = Work 2 sc in the next st.
Invdec (invisible single crochet decrease) = Insert hook in front loop only of each of next 2 sts, yo and draw through both sts, yo and draw through 2 loops on hook—1 st decreased.

GAUGE
28 sc and 28 rnds = 4 in. / 10 cm in sc
Gauge is not critical for this project. Ensure your stitches are tight so the stuffing won't show through.

NOTES

- Work in continuous rounds unless otherwise indicated.
- When indicated, join at the end of a round with a slip stitch in the first stitch. To join new yarn to a stitch, insert hook in stitch and pull up a loop in indicated color.
- To change colors, work the last yarn over of the previous stitch with the new color. Fasten off previous color unless otherwise indicated.
- If desired, instead of making a magic ring, chain 2 and work indicated stitches in the 2nd chain from the hook.

Fun Fact

According to Director Henry Selick, Oogie Boogie was "the toughest" character to design for *Tim Burton's The Nightmare Before Christmas.*

Feet (Make 2)

With **A** make a magic ring.

Rnd 1: 3 sc in magic ring—3 sc.

Rnd 2: Inc, sc 2—4 sc.

Rnd 3: [Inc, sc] around—6 sc.

Rnds 4–5: Sc around.

Rnd 6: [Inc, sc] around—9 sc.

Rnd 7: [Inc, sc 2] around—12 sc.

Rnd 8: Ch 6, skip next 6 sts (*leg opening made*), sc 6—6 sc.

Rnd 9: Sc in each st and ch around, join—12 sc.

Fasten off leaving a long tail for sewing. Using tail, pinch Foot closed and sew 6 sts together through both thicknesses to create a finished straight seam at back of heel. Weave in ends.

Continue to Leg.

Legs (Make 2)

With **A** join to first unworked st of Rnd 7 of Foot.

Rnd 1: Ch 1, sc 6, sc in gap at side of Foot before underside of next 6 chs, sc in next 6 chs, sc in gap at side of Foot before first sc, join—14 sc.

Rnd 2: Ch 1, [inc, sc 6] around, join—16 sc.

Rnd 3: Ch 1, [inc, sc 7] around, join—18 sc.

Rnd 4: Ch 1, sc around, join.

On first Leg, place st marker in 9th st. Fasten off first Leg, do not fasten off 2nd Leg. Stuff Legs. Continue to Body.

Body

With **A**.

Rnd 1: Ch 12, sc in marked st of first Leg, sc around first Leg, sc in 12 chs from beginning of rnd, sc around 2nd Leg, sc 12 in underside of same 12 chs—60 sc.

Rnd 2: [Inc, sc 9] around—66 sc.

Rnd 3: [Sc 5, inc, sc 5] around—72 sc.

Rnds 4–20: Sc around.

Rnd 21: [Sc 11, invdec, sc 11] around—69 sc.

Rnd 22: [Invdec, sc 21] around—66 sc.

Rnd 23: [Sc 10, invdec, sc 10] around—63 sc.

Rnd 24: [Invdec, sc 19] around—60 sc.

Insert styrofoam ball, do not stuff Body with stuffing.

Rnd 25: [Sc 9, invdec, sc 9] around—57 sc.

Rnd 26: [Invdec, sc 17] around—54 sc.

Rnd 27: [Sc 8, invdec, sc 8] around—51 sc.

Rnd 28: [Invdec, sc 15] around—48 sc.

Using st markers, mark 6 sts for each armhole at either side of Body, with st marker in first and 6th st. Ensure there are 18 sts at front of Body and 18 sts at back of Body between markers.

Rnd 29: Sc around to first marked st, ch 6, skip 6 marked sts (*armhole made*), sc around to next marked st, ch 6, skipped 6 marked sts (*armhole made*), sc in remaining sts around—36 sc, 12 chs.

Rnd 30: Sc in each st and ch around—48 sc.

Rnd 31: [Sc 3, invdec, sc 3] around—42 sc.

Rnd 32: [Invdec, sc 5] around—36 sc.
Rnd 33: [Sc 2, invdec, sc 2] around—30 sc.
Rnd 34: [Invdec, sc 3] around—24 sc.
Rnd 35: Inc around—48 sc.
Rnd 36: [Inc, sc 7] around—54 sc.
Using st markers mark 27 center front sts for Mouth with marker in first and last st, leaving 27 sts for back of Head.
Rnd 37: Sc around to first marked st, ch 27, skip 27 marked sts (*mouth opening made*), sc in remaining sts around—27 sc.
Rnd 38: Sc in each ch and st around—54 sc.
Rnd 39: [Invdec, sc 7] around—48 sc.
Rnd 40: [Sc 7, invdec, sc 7] around—45 sc.
Rnd 41: [Invdec, sc 13] around—42 sc.
Rnd 42: [Sc 6, invdec, sc 6] around—39 sc.
Rnd 43: [Invdec, sc 11] around—36 sc.
Rnd 44: [Sc 5, invdec, sc 5] around—33 sc.
Rnd 45: [Invdec, sc 9] around—30 sc.
Rnd 46: [Sc 4, invdec, sc 4] around—27 sc.
Rnd 47: [Invdec, sc 7] around—24 sc.
Rnd 48: Sc around.
Rnd 49: [Sc 3, invdec, sc 3] around—21 sc.
Rnd 50: Sc around.
Rnd 51: [Invdec, sc 5] around—18 sc.
Rnd 52: Sc around.
Rnd 53: [Sc 2, invdec, sc 2] around—15 sc.
Rnd 54: Sc around.
Rnd 55: [Invdec, sc 3] around—12 sc.
Rnd 56: Sc around.
Rnd 57: [Sc, invdec, sc] around—9 sc.
Rnd 58: Sc around.
Rnd 59: [Invdec, sc] around—6 sc.
Rnd 60: Sc around.
Rnd 61: Invdec, sc 4—5 sc.
Rnd 62: Invdec, sc 3—4 sc.
Fasten off, weave in end.

Mouth

With **B** make a magic ring.
Rnd 1: 6 sc in ring—6 sc.
Rnd 2: Inc around—12 sc.
Rnd 3: [Inc, sc] around—18 sc.
Rnd 4: [Sc, inc, sc] around—24 sc.
Rnd 5: [Inc, sc 3] around—30 sc.
Rnd 6: [Sc 2, inc, sc 2] around—36 sc.
Rnd 7: [Inc, sc 5] around—42 sc.
Rnd 8: [Sc 3, inc, sc 3] around—48 sc.
Rnd 9: [Inc, sc 7] around—54 sc.
Fasten off, leaving a long tail for sewing. Stuff top of Head very lightly, but do not stuff bottom of Head. Insert Mouth into mouth opening of Head and use tail to sew Mouth in place. Weave in ends.

Eyebrows (Make 2)

With **A**.
Row 1: Ch 10.
Fasten off, leaving a long tail for sewing.

Arms (Make 2)

With **A** join to first skipped st of Rnd 28 of Body.
Rnd 1: Ch 1, sc 6 on Rnd 28 of Body, sc in gap before underside of next 6 chs, sc in next 6 chs, sc in gap before first sc, join—14 sc.
Rnd 2: Sc around.
Rnds 3–6: Invdec, sc around—10 sc at end of Rnd 6.
Stuff arm.
Rnds 7–12: Invdec, sc around—4 sc at end of Rnd 12.
Fasten off, leaving a long tail for sewing. Sew remaining 4 sts closed. Weave in end.

Finishing

Using black felt, cut 2 half-circles and glue in place between Rnds 42 and 45 of Head. Sew Eyebrows above eye using photo as a guide. Using black embroidery thread and photo as a guide, embroider stitch details from tip of Foot and up the side of the Foot. Continue stitching up side of Body to armpit, and up to tip of Arm. Repeat on opposite side. Curl top of Body and sew in place. Weave in end.

Tamatoa

Designed by Lee Sartori

Skill Level: Intermediate

He collects all things shiny and valuable, tucks his treasures away in his remote cave, and exudes beauty. We're talking about Tamatoa, the giant crab, of course! Who did you expect? Living in The Realm of Monsters, Tamatoa doesn't get many visitors who might appreciate his hoard of jewels and trinkets. That might be because he'd have no qualms about eating intruders. So when Moana, a daring way-finder, has the audacity to break into his cave, Tamatoa is angry. He's also none too pleased with Moana's companion, legendary demigod Maui. And he has every right to be. As far as Tamatoa is concerned, he stole Maui's magical hook fair and square. But now that Moana and Maui are here to get it back, Tamatoa might as well show off some of his amazing vocal skills and entertain his guests. It also happens to be a great way to distract them while he inevitably captures and eats them!

Tamatoa wants nothing more than to be positively coated in treasure, and we imagine that would carry over into a crocheted version of him, too. If you find any baubles or trinkets around, be sure to add them to *your* Tamatoa. The shinier the better, so he feels right at home.

"Are you just trying to get me to talk about myself? Because if you are . . . I will gladly do so . . . in song form!"

—Tamatoa, *Moana* (2016)

YARN

Worsted weight (#4 medium) yarn, shown in WeCrochet Swish (100% fine super-wash merino wool, 110 yd. / 100 m per 1.75 oz. / 50 g ball)

Color A: Dijon, 1 ball
Color B: Amethyst Heather, 1 ball
Color C: Allium, 1 ball
Color D: Phoenix, 1 ball
Color E: California Poppy, 1 ball
Color F: White, 1 ball

HOOK

US D (3.25 mm) crochet hook

NOTIONS

Black embroidery thread
Pair of 6 mm black safety eyes
Gold buttons, sequins, and trinkets
Glue
White felt
Black felt
Blue eyeshadow
Stitch marker
Polyester stuffing
Yarn needle
Scissors

FINISHED MEASUREMENTS

Height: 4" / 10 cm
Width: 10" / 25 cm

SPECIAL STITCHES

Inc (increase) = Work 2 sc in the next st.

Invdec (invisible single crochet decrease) = Insert hook in front loop only of each of next 2 sts, yo and draw through both sts, yo and draw through 2 loops on hook—1 st decreased.

GAUGE

28 sc and 28 rnds = 4 in. / 10 cm in sc

Gauge is not critical for this project. Ensure your stitches are tight so the stuffing won't show through.

NOTES

- Work in continuous rounds unless otherwise indicated.
- When indicated, join at the end of a round with a slip stitch in the first stitch. To join new yarn to a stitch, insert hook in stitch and pull up a loop in indicated color.
- To change colors, work the last yarn over of the previous stitch with the new color. Fasten off previous color unless otherwise indicated.
- If desired, instead of making a magic ring, chain 2 and work indicated stitches in the 2nd chain from the hook.

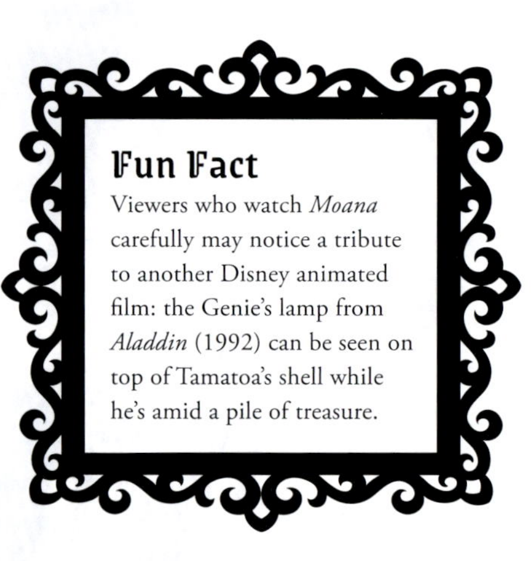

Fun Fact

Viewers who watch *Moana* carefully may notice a tribute to another Disney animated film: the Genie's lamp from *Aladdin* (1992) can be seen on top of Tamatoa's shell while he's amid a pile of treasure.

Shell Top

With **A** make a magic ring.
Rnd 1: 6 sc in ring—6 sc.
Rnd 2: Inc around—12 sc.
Rnd 3: [Inc, sc] around—18 sc.
Rnd 4: [Sc, inc, sc] around—24 sc.
Rnd 5: [Inc, sc 3] around—30 sc.
Rnd 6: [Sc 2, inc, 2 sc] around—36 sc.
Rnd 7: [Inc, sc 5] around—42 sc.
Rnd 8: [Sc 3, inc, sc 3] around—48 sc.
Rnd 9: [Inc, sc 7] around—54 sc.
Change to **B**.
Rnd 10: Ch 1, working in BLO, [sc 4, inc, sc 4] around, join—60 sc.
Rnds 11–14: Sc around.
Fasten off, leaving a long tail for sewing.

Shell Bottom

With **C** make a magic ring.
Rnds 1–9: Repeat Rnds 1–9 of Shell Top.
Rnd 10: [Sc 4, inc, sc 4] around—60 sc.
Rnd 11: Sc around.
Fasten off, leaving a long tail for sewing. Sew Shell Bottom to Shell Top, stuffing as you sew. Weave in ends.

Head

With **D** make a magic ring.
Rnd 1: 6 sc in ring—6 sc.
Rnd 2: Inc around—12 sc.
Rnd 3: [Inc, sc] around—18 sc.
Rnd 4: [Sc, inc, sc] around—24 sc.
Rnds 5–6: Sc around.
Change to **E**.
Rnd 7: Ch 1, working in BLO, sc around, join.

Rnds 8–10: Ch 1, sc around, join.
Change to **C**.
Rnds 11–12: Ch 1, sc around, join.
Rnd 13: Ch 1, [sc, invdec, sc] around, join—18 sc.
Rnd 14: Ch 1, [invdec, sc] around, join—12 sc.
Rnd 15: Ch 1, sc around, join.
Change to **B**. Stuff Head and continue stuffing as work progresses.
Rnd 16: Ch 1, sc around, join.
Rnd 17: Ch 1, [invdec, sc] around, join—8 sc.
Rnd 18: Ch 1, invdec around, join—4 sc.
Fasten off leaving a long tail for sewing. Sew remaining 4 sts closed. Weave in end.

Inner Eyes (Make 2)

With **F** make a magic ring.
Rnd 1: 6 sc in ring, join—6 sc.
Fasten off leaving a long tail for sewing.

Outer Eyes (Make 2)

With **C** make a magic ring.
Rnd 1: 6 sc in ring—6 sc.
Rnd 2: Inc around—12 sc.
Rnd 3: Sc around.
Fasten off, leaving a long tail for sewing. Sew Inner Eye to middle of Outer Eye. Insert safety eye into center of Eye through both thicknesses. Sew Eyes to sides of Head. Weave in ends.

Antennae (Make 2)

With **C**.
Row 1: Ch 40 tightly.
Fasten off. Sew to back of Head behind Eyes. Weave in ends.

Curved Claw (Make 2)

With **E** make a magic ring.
Rnd 1: Ch 1, 3 sc in ring, join—3 sc.
Rnd 2: Ch 1, inc, sc 2, join—4 sc.
Rnd 3: Ch 1, inc 2, sc 2, join—6 sc.
Rnd 4: Ch 1, inc 2, sc around, join—8 sc.
Rnds 5–12: Repeat Rnd 4—24 sc at end of Rnd 12.
Rnd 13: Ch 1, sc around, join.
Fasten off. Stuff.

Straight Claw (Make 2)

With **E** make a magic ring.
Rnd 1: 3 sc in ring—3 sc.
Rnd 2: Inc, sc 2—4 sc.
Rnd 3: [Inc, sc] around—6 sc.
Rnd 4: [Sc, inc, sc] around—8 sc.
Rnd 5: [Inc, sc 3] around—10 sc.
Rnd 6: [Sc 2, inc, sc 2] around—12 sc.
Rnd 7: [Inc, sc 5] around—14 sc.
Rnd 8: [Sc 3, inc, sc 3] around—16 sc.
Rnd 9: [Inc, sc 7] around—18 sc.
Rnd 10: [Sc 4, inc, sc 4] around—20 sc.
Rnd 11: [Inc, sc 9] around—22 sc.
Rnd 12: [Sc 5, inc, sc 5] around—24 sc.
Stuff. Do not fasten off. Continue to Arm.

Arms (Make 2)

Continuing with **E**.

Rnd 1 (joining): Sc in sc on inside edge of Curved Claw, sc 23 around Curved Claw, sc 24 around Straight Claw—48 sc.

Change to **D**.

Rnds 2–6: Ch 1, sc around, join.

Rnd 7: Ch 1, [sc 7, invdec, sc 7] around, join—45 sc.

Rnd 8: Ch 1, [invdec, sc 13] around, join—42 sc.

Rnd 9: Ch 1, [sc 6, invdec, sc 6] around, join—39 sc.

Change to **B**.

Rnd 10: Ch 1, [invdec, sc 11] around, join—36 sc.

Rnd 11: Ch 1, [sc 5, invdec, sc 5] around, join—33 sc.

Rnd 12: Ch 1, [invdec, sc 9] around, join—30 sc.

Rnd 13: Ch 1, [sc 4, invdec, sc 4] around, join—27 sc.

Rnd 14: Ch 1, [invdec, sc 7] around, join—24 sc.

Rnd 15: Ch 1, [sc 3, invdec, sc 3] around, join—21 sc.

Rnd 16: Ch 1, [invdec, sc 5] around, join—18 sc.

Rnd 17: Ch 1, sc around, join.

Change to **C**.

Rnds 18–22: Ch 1, sc around, join.

Rnd 23: Ch 1, [sc 2, invdec, sc 2] around, join—15 sc.

Rnds 24–28: Ch 1, sc around, join.

Rnd 29: Ch 1, [invdec, sc 3] around, join—12 sc.

Rnds 30–34: Ch 1, sc around, join.

Fasten off leaving a long tail for sewing. Stuff Arm. Sew Arms to Body at joining seam between Top and Bottom Shells, and on either side of Head.

Arm Detail 1 (Make 2)

With **B**.

Row 1: Ch 18.

Fasten off, leaving a long tail for sewing. Sew to Rnd 18 of Arm. Weave in ends.

Arm Detail 2 (Make 2)

With **B**.

Row 1: Ch 36.

Fasten off, leaving a long tail for sewing. Sew to Rnd 10 of Arm. Weave in ends.

Back Legs (Make 3)

With **B** make a magic ring.

Rnd 1: 3 sc in ring—3 sc.

Rnd 2: Inc, sc 2—4 sc.

Rnd 3: [Inc, sc] around—6 sc.

Rnd 4: [Sc, inc, sc] around—8 sc.

Rnd 5: [Inc, sc 3] around—10 sc.

Rnd 6: [Sc 2, inc, sc 2] around—12 sc.

Rnd 7: [Inc, sc 5] around—14 sc.
Rnd 8: Working in FLO sc around, join.
Rnd 9: Ch 1, working in unworked BL of Rnd 7, [inc, sc 6] around—16 sc.
Rnd 10: [Inc, sc 7] around—18 sc.
Rnds 11–15: Sc around.
Rnd 16: Working in BLO sc 9, working in both loops sc 9.
Rnds 17–19: Sc around.
Rnd 20: Sc in 9 unworked FL on Rnd 15, skip 9 sts on current rnd, sc 9 on current rnd—18 sc.
Rnds 21–25: Sc around.
Rnd 26: [Sc 2, invdec, sc 2] around—15 sc.
Rnds 27–31: Sc around.
Rnd 32: [Invdec, sc 3] around—12 sc.
Rnds 33–37: Sc around.
Fasten off, leaving a long tail for sewing. Stuff.

Broken Leg

With **B**, ch 18, being careful not to twist, sl st in first ch to form a ring.
Rnd 1: Ch 1, sc in each ch around, join—18 sc.
Rnds 2–23: Repeat Rnds 11—32 of Back Leg.
Fasten off, leaving a long tail for sewing. Do not stuff. Sew last rnd of Broken Leg to front left of Body. Sew Back Leg behind Broken Leg. Sew remaining 2 Back Legs to opposite side of Body.

Leg Detail (Make 4)

With **B**.
Row 1: Ch 18.
Fasten off, leaving a long tail for sewing. Sew detail around middle of Leg at bends at Rnd 10 on Legs and Rnd 12 on Broken Leg. Weave in ends.

Denticles (Make 2)

With **F**.
Row 1: Ch 2, sc in 2nd ch, [ch 3, sc in 2nd ch from hook, skip last ch] 9 times—10 sc.
Fasten off, leaving a long tail for sewing. Sew to inside of claw using photos as a guide.

Finishing

Using glue, secure gold buttons, sequins, and trinkets to top of shell. Using photo as a guide, cut a half circle from black felt for mouth. Using white felt, cut individual teeth and glue to mouth shape. Glue mouth to face. Using blue eyeshadow, add blue shading at each rnd where 2 colors change.

Part 3

Magical Mischief-Makers

Ursula

Designed by Lee Sartori

Skill Level: Intermediate

Life under the sea is such a drag! That's according to the curious and rebellious young mermaid Ariel, daughter of the sea king. When Ariel's inquisitiveness steers her to the human world of sunshine and open land, Ariel falls for a handsome human prince. Interactions with humans are strictly forbidden in the kingdom, so Ariel is forced to make a dangerous deal with the sea witch Ursula: Ursula agrees to turn Ariel human for three days . . . in exchange for the princess's voice. Through her tempting music, magnificent shape-shifting, and devious scheming, Ursula sabotages Ariel's plans at every opportunity. Though her own schemes are much grander: She'd rather see herself on the throne than King Triton. Ultimate power over the sea might be within Ursula's cunning grasp, if only true love would stop getting in the way.

Ursula the sea witch is not your average crochet doll! Fantastic white hair and long, luxurious tentacles set this villain apart from the pack! And don't forget to include Ursula's little magical shell necklace where she keeps Ariel's voice trapped! It's the key to Triton's undoing . . .

"Flotsam! Jetsam! I want you to keep an extra close watch on this pretty little daughter of his. She may be the key to Triton's undoing."

—Ursula, *The Little Mermaid* (1989)

YARN

Worsted weight (#4 medium) yarn, shown in WeCrochet Swish (100% fine superwash merino wool, 110 yd. / 100 m per 1.75 oz. / 50 g ball)

Color A: Dove Heather, 1 ball
Color B: Black, 2 balls
Color C: Karma Heather, 1 ball
Color D: Denim, 1 ball
Color E: White, 1 ball
Color F: Dijon, 1 ball

HOOK

US D (3.25 mm) crochet hook

NOTIONS

Black embroidery thread
Pair of 9 mm black safety eyes
Stitch marker
Polyester stuffing
Yarn needle
Scissors

FINISHED MEASUREMENTS

Height: 9" / 22.5 cm
Width: 11" / 27.5 cm

SPECIAL STITCHES

Cluster (3-dc cluster) = [Yo, insert hook in indicated st, yo and draw up a loop, yo and draw through 2 loops] 3 times, yo and draw through all loops on hook.

Inc (increase) = Work 2 sc in the next st.

Invdec (invisible single crochet decrease) = Insert hook in FLO of each of next 2 sts, yo and draw through both sts, yo and draw through 2 loops on hook—1 st decreased.

Popcorn (popcorn stitch) = Work 5 dc in next st, drop loop on hook, insert hook from front to back in first dc made, place dropped loop on hook and draw through dc.

GAUGE

28 sc and 28 rnds = 4 in. / 10 cm in sc

Gauge is not critical for this project. Ensure your stitches are tight so the stuffing won't show through.

NOTES

- Work in continuous rounds unless otherwise indicated.
- When indicated, join at the end of a round with a slip stitch in the first stitch. To join new yarn to a stitch, insert hook in stitch and pull up a loop in indicated color.
- To change colors, work the last yarn over of the previous stitch with the new color. Fasten off previous color unless otherwise indicated.
- If desired, instead of making a magic ring, chain 2 and work indicated stitches in the 2nd chain from the hook.

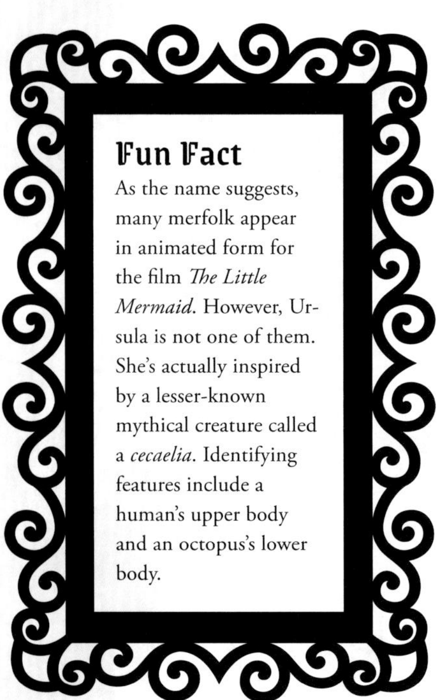

Fun Fact

As the name suggests, many merfolk appear in animated form for the film *The Little Mermaid*. However, Ursula is not one of them. She's actually inspired by a lesser-known mythical creature called a *cecaelia*. Identifying features include a human's upper body and an octopus's lower body.

Arms (Make 2)

With **A**, make a magic ring.
Rnd 1: 6 sc in ring—6 sc.
Rnd 2: Inc around—12 sc.
Rnds 3–4: Sc around.
Rnd 5: Popcorn, sc 11.
Rnds 6–7: Sc around.
Rnd 8: Invdec around—6 sc.
Rnd 9: [Inc, sc] around—9 sc.
Rnd 10: [Sc, inc, sc] around—12 sc.
Rnd 11: [Inc, sc 3] around—15 sc.
Rnds 12–21: Sc around.
Fasten off. Stuff. Set Arms aside to join to Body.

Tentacles (Make 6)

With **B** make a magic ring. Stuff Tentacles as work progresses.
Rnd 1: 3 sc in ring—3 sc.
Rnds 2–10: Inc, sc around—12 sc at end of Rnd 10.
Begin working in rows.
Row 11 (WS): Ch 1 tightly, turn, sc 6, leave remaining 6 sts unworked—6 sc.
Begin working in rnds.
Rnd 12 (RS): Ch 1 tightly, turn, sc 6, sc in next 6 unworked sts of Rnd 10—12 sc.
Rnd 13: Sc around.
Begin working in rows.
Row 14: Sc 6, turn leaving remaining 6 sts unworked—6 sc.
Row 15 (WS): Ch 1 tightly, sc across, turn.
Begin working in rnds.
Rnd 16 (RS): Ch 1 tightly, sc 6, sc in next 6 unworked sts of Rnd 13—12 sc.
Rnd 17: Sc around.
Row/Rnds 15–49: Rep Row 14–Rnd 17 eight times.
Rnds 50–57: Sc around.
Rnd 58: [Inc, sc 3] around—15 sc.
Rnds 59–62: Sc around.
Rnd 63: [Sc 2, inc, sc 2] around—18 sc.
Rnds 64–65: Sc around.
Fasten off.

Body

The next round will join each of the Tentacles together. With **B** join in any st of one Tentacle.
Rnd 1: Sc 9 on first Tentacle, leaving remaining 9 sts unworked, *holding next Tentacle in line with sts, sc 9 on next Tentacle, leaving remaining 9 sts unworked; repeat from * until all Tentacles are joined—54 sc on Body, 9 unworked sc on each Tentacle.
Rnds 2–5: Sc around—54 sc.
Rnd 6: [Sc, inc, sc] around—72 sc.
Rnds 7–10: Sc around.
Rnd 11: [Sc 5, invdec, sc 5] around—66 sc.
Rnd 12: [Invdec, sc 9] around—60 sc.
Rnd 13: [Sc 4, invdec, sc 4] around—54 sc.
Rnds 14–15: Sc around.
Change to **D**.
Rnd 16: Ch 1, working in BLO sc around, join.
Change to **A**.

Rnd 17: Ch 1, working in BLO sc around, join.

Hold Arms in line with Body to join on next rnd.

Rnd 18: Ch 1, sc 14 on Body, sc 15 around first Arm, sc 27 on Body, sc 15 around 2nd Arm, sc 13 on Body, join—84 sc.

Rnd 19: [Sc 6, invdec, sc 6] around—78 sc.

Rnd 20: [Invdec, sc 11] around—72 sc.

Rnd 21: [Sc 5, invdec, sc 5] around—66 sc.

Rnd 22: [Invdec, sc 9] around—60 sc.

Rnd 23: [Sc 4, invdec, sc 4] around—54 sc.

Rnd 24: [Invdec, sc 7] around—48 sc.

Rnd 25: [Sc 3, invdec, sc 3] around—42 sc.

Rnd 26: [Invdec, sc 5] around—36 sc.

Rnd 27: [Sc 2, invdec, sc 2] around—30 sc.

Rnd 28: [Invdec, sc 3] around—24 sc.

Stuff Body and shoulders firmly.

Rnd 29: 3 sc in each st around—72 sc.

Rnds 30–34: Sc around.

Rnd 35: [Sc 11, invdec, sc 11] around—69 sc.

Rnd 36: [Invdec, sc 21] around—66 sc.

Rnd 37: [Sc 10, invdec, sc 10] around—63 sc.

"Yes, hurry home, Princess. We wouldn't want to miss old Daddy's celebration, now, would we? Ha! Celebration, indeed. Oh, bah! In my day, we had fantastical feasts when I lived in the palace. And now look at me. Wasted away to practically nothing. Banished and exiled and practically starving, while he and his flimsy fish folk celebrate. Well, I'll give 'em something to celebrate soon enough."

—Ursula, *The Little Mermaid* (1989)

Rnd 38: [Invdec, sc 19] around—60 sc.
Rnd 39: [Sc 9, invdec, sc 9] around—57 sc.
Rnd 40: [Invdec, sc 17] around—54 sc.
Rnd 41: [Invdec, sc 7] around—48 sc.
Rnds 42–45: Sc around.
Rnd 46: [Sc 3, invdec, sc 3] around—42 sc.
Add safety eyes between Rnds 42 and 43, approximately 7 sts apart. Using a length of **D**, add eye detail over each eye. Using a length of **B**, add 2 eyelashes at sides of each eye. Using a length of **A** held double, embroider nose between Rnds 41 and 42 across 4 sts. Stuff Head and continue stuffing as work progresses.
Rnd 47: [Invdec, sc 5] around—36 sc.
Rnd 48: [Sc 2, invdec, sc 2] around—30 sc.
Rnd 49: [Invdec, sc 3] around—24 sc.
Rnd 50: [Sc, invdec, sc] around—18 sc.
Rnd 51: [Invdec, sc] around—12 sc.
Rnd 52: Invdec around—6 sc.
Fasten off leaving a long tail for sewing. Sew remaining 6 sts closed. Weave in end.

Bottom

With **C**, join to first unworked st of any Tentacle.
Rnd 1: Ch 1, *sc in 9 skipped sts, work a decrease between Tentacles by inserting hook into side of first Tentacle, yo and draw up a loop, insert hook in gap between Tentacles, yo and draw up a loop, insert hook into side of next Tentacle, yo and draw up a loop, yo and draw through all loops on hook; repeat from * around—60 sc.
Rnd 2: Working in BLO, sc around.
Rnd 3: [Sc 4, invdec, sc 4] around—54 sc.
Rnd 4: [Invdec, sc 7] around—48 sc.
Rnd 5: [Sc 3, invdec, sc 3] around—42 sc.
Rnd 6: [Invdec, sc 5] around—36 sc.
Rnd 7: [Sc 2, invdec, sc 2] around—30 sc.
Stuff lower Body and tops of Tentacles if needed.
Rnd 8: [Invdec, sc 3] around—24 sc.
Rnd 9: [Sc, invdec, sc] around—18 sc.
Rnd 10: [Invdec, sc] around—12 sc.
Rnd 11: Invdec around—6 sc.
Fasten off leaving a long tail for sewing. Sew remaining 6 sts closed. Weave in end.

Bodice (Make 2)

With **B**.
Row 1: Ch 2, 3 sc in 2nd ch from hook, turn—3 sc.
Row 2: Ch 1, inc across—6 sc.
Join **D** in first st of Row 2 in BL.
Row 3: Ch 1, working in BLO, sc across.

Fasten off leaving a long tail for sewing. Sew to front center 13 sts of Body lining up Row 3 of Bodice with Rnd 16 of Body. Weave in ends.

Ears (Make 2)

With **A** make a magic ring.
Rnd 1: 5 sc in ring—5 sc.
Fasten off leaving a long tail for sewing. Sew Ears to sides of Head in line with nose.

Hair Crown

With **E** make a magic ring.
Rnd 1: 6 sc in ring—6 sc.
Rnd 2: Inc around—12 sc.
Rnd 3: [Inc, sc] around—18 sc.
Rnd 4: [Sc, inc, sc] around—24 sc.
Rnd 5: [Inc, sc 3] around—30 sc.
Rnd 6: [Sc 2, inc, sc 2] around—36 sc.
Rnd 7: [Inc, sc 5] around—42 sc.
Rnd 8: [Sc 3, inc, sc 3] around—48 sc.
Rnd 9: Sc, hdc, 2 dc in next st, hdc, sc 43, sl st—48 sts.
Begin working in rows.
Row 10: Turn, skip first sc, sc 41, sl st, turn leaving remaining sts unworked—41 sc.
Row 11: Skip first sc, sc 39, sl st, turn—39 sc.
Row 12: Skip first sc, sc 37, sl st, turn—37 sc.
Row 13: Skip first sc, sc 35, sl st, turn—35 sc.
Row 14: Skip first sc, sc 33, sl st, turn—33 sc.
Rnd 15: Ch 1, sc around entire piece evenly.
Fasten off, leaving a long tail for sewing. Sew Hair Crown to top of Head. Weave in end.

Hair (Make 8)

With **E**.
Row 1 (first strand): Ch 10, sl st in 2nd ch from hook, sc 2, hdc 3, dc 3—9 sts.
Rows 2–5 (remaining strands): Ch 11, starting in 2nd ch from hook, sl st, sc 2, hdc 3, dc 3, leave last ch unworked—9 sts.
Fasten off leaving a long tail for sewing. Starting at front hairline, sew a strip of hair across top of Head. Add a new strip of hair behind first and continue going back for remaining strips of hair. Weave in ends.

Earrings (Make 2)

With **C**.
Rnd 1: Ch 3, sc in 2nd ch from hook, 3 sc in next, rotate to work in underside of ch, sl st, sl st in skipped ch—4 sc.
Fasten off, leaving a long tail for sewing. Sew to bottom of each Ear. Weave in ends.

Shell Necklace Charm

With **F**.
Rnd 1: Ch 12, starting in 2nd ch from hook 3 sc in next 9 chs, sl st 2.
Fasten off, leaving a long tail for sewing. Using a strand of **B**, add a necklace around neck. Sew Shell Necklace Charm to center front of necklace. Weave in ends.

Tentacle Details (Make 6)
With **C** leave a long tail at start for sewing.
Row 1: Ch 41, starting in 2nd ch from hook sc across, turn—40 sc.
Row 2: Ch 1, [sc 2, cluster, sc 2] across, turn.
Row 3: Ch 1, sc across.
Fasten off, leaving a long tail for sewing. Sew each Tentacle Detail to bottom of a Tentacle. Weave in ends.

Hades

Designed by Lee Sartori

Skill Level: Easy

In a jealous bid to destroy a golden legacy, Hades, god of the Underworld, hatches a plot to turn his nephew Hercules into a mere mortal. As it goes with many villainous schemes, Hades's plot isn't really about Hercules, it's about the boy's father, Zeus. At first, everything seems to be going close enough to plan, with Hercules half mortal and banished from Zeus's kingdom. Unfortunately for Hades, Hercules is presented with a magical loophole: He can return to his father's kingdom on Mount Olympus and take his place among the gods if he finds a way to become a "true hero." That means Hades must stop Hercules from doing anything truly heroic, even if it means teaming up with the powerful Titans and destroying everything between Mount Olympus and the Underworld that gets in his way.

Watch out! When Hades gets angry (and, wow, does he get angry!) his blue-flame hair flares up with the heat of his fury! Luckily for us, our little crochet Hades doesn't give off any heat, although his flaming hair does indicate that Hades is in a foul mood indeed!

"I've got 24 hours to get rid of this bozo, or the entire scheme I've been setting up for 18 years goes up in smoke, and you are wearing his merchandise?"

—Hades addressing Pain, *Hercules* (1997)

YARN

Worsted weight (#4 medium) yarn, shown in WeCrochet Swish (100% fine super-wash merino wool, 110 yd. / 100 m per 1.75 oz. / 50 g ball)

Color A: Dove Heather, 1 ball
Color B: Marble Heather, 1 ball
Color C: Black, 1 ball
Color D: Electric Blue, 1 ball
Color E: Artic Heather, 1 ball

HOOK

US D (3.25 mm) crochet hook

NOTIONS

Pair of 12 mm yellow-and-black safety eyes
Black embroidery thread
Stitch marker
Polyester stuffing
Yarn needle
Scissors

FINISHED MEASUREMENTS

Height: 13" / 32.5 cm
Width: 8" / 20 cm

SPECIAL STITCHES

Inc (increase) = Work 2 sc in the next st.

Invdec (invisible single crochet decrease) = Insert hook in front loop only of each of next 2 sts, yo and draw through both sts, yo and draw through 2 loops on hook—1 st decreased.

Popcorn (popcorn stitch) = Work 5 dc in next st, drop loop on hook, insert hook from front to back in first dc made, place dropped loop on hook and draw through dc.

Sc2tog (single crochet 2 together) = [Insert hook in next st, yo and draw up a loop] twice, yo and draw through all loops on hook—1 st decreased.

GAUGE

28 sc and 28 rnds = 4 in. / 10 cm in sc

Gauge is not critical for this project. Ensure your stitches are tight so the stuffing won't show through.

NOTES

- Work in continuous rounds unless otherwise indicated.
- When indicated, join at the end of a round with a slip stitch in the first stitch. To join new yarn to a stitch, insert hook in stitch and pull up a loop in indicated color.
- To change colors, work the last yarn over of the previous stitch with the new color. Fasten off previous color unless otherwise indicated.
- If desired, instead of making a magic ring, chain 2 and work indicated stitches in the 2nd chain from the hook.

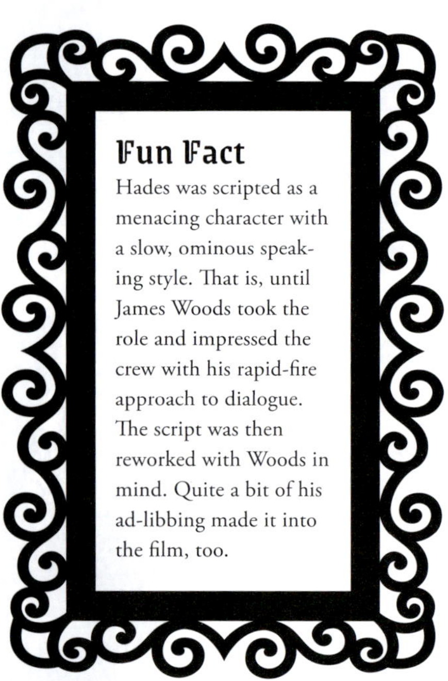

Fun Fact

Hades was scripted as a menacing character with a slow, ominous speaking style. That is, until James Woods took the role and impressed the crew with his rapid-fire approach to dialogue. The script was then reworked with Woods in mind. Quite a bit of his ad-libbing made it into the film, too.

Arms (Make 2)

With **A**, make a magic ring.
Rnd 1: 6 sc in ring—6 sc.
Rnd 2: Inc around—12 sc.
Rnds 3–4: Sc around.
Rnd 5: Popcorn, sc 11.
Rnds 6–7: Sc around.
Rnd 8: Inc, sc around—13 sc.
Rnd 9: Sc around.
Rnd 10: Inc, sc around—14 sc.
Rnd 11: Sc around.
Rnd 12: Inc, sc around—15 sc.
Rnds 13–15: Sc around.
Change to **B**.
Rnd 16: Ch 1, working in BLO sc around, join—15 sc.
Rnd 17: Ch 1, working in FLO sc around, join.
Rnd 18: Ch 1, working in unworked BLO of Rnd 16 sc around, join.
Fasten off. Stuff. Set Arms aside to join to Upper Body.

Lower Body

With **C**, make a magic ring.
Rnd 1: 6 sc in ring—6 sc.
Rnd 2: Inc around—12 sc.
Rnd 3: [Inc, sc] around—18 sc.
Rnd 4: [Sc, inc, sc] around—24 sc.
Rnd 5: [Inc, sc 3] around—30 sc.
Rnd 6: [Sc 2, inc, sc 2] around—36 sc.
Rnd 7: [Inc, sc 5] around—42 sc.
Rnd 8: [Sc 3, inc, sc 3] around—48 sc.
Rnd 9: [Inc, sc 7] around—54 sc.
Rnd 10: Working in BLO sc around.
Rnds 11–22: Sc around.
Rnd 23: [Sc 8, invdec, sc 8] around—51 sc.
Rnd 24: Sc around.
Rnd 25: [Invdec, sc 15] around—48 sc.
Rnd 26: Sc around.
Rnd 27: [Sc 7, invdec, sc 7] around—45 sc.
Rnd 28: Sc around.
Rnd 29: [Invdec, sc 13] around—42 sc.
Rnd 30: Sc around.
Rnd 31: [Sc 6, invdec, sc 6] around—39 sc.
Rnd 32: Sc around.
Rnd 33: [Invdec, sc 11] around—36 sc.
Rnd 34: Sc around.
Change to **B**. Stuff.

Upper Body

Continue with **B**.
Rnd 1: Ch 1, working in BLO, sc around, join—36 sc.
Rnd 2: Ch 1 tightly, [inc, sc 11] around, do not join—39 sc.
Rnd 3: [Sc 6, inc, sc 6] around—42 sc.
Rnd 4: [Inc, sc 13] around—45 sc.
Rnd 5: [Sc 7, inc, sc 7] around—48 sc.
Rnd 6: [Inc, sc 15] around—51 sc.
Rnd 7: [Sc 8, inc, sc 8] around—54 sc.
Using 2 st markers mark 1 st for armpits on each side of Upper Body leaving 26 sts for front of Body, and 26 sts for back of Body between marked sts. Hold Arms in line with Body to join on next rnd.
Rnd 8: Sc around to first marked st on Body, sc in marked st, sc 15 around first Arm, sc around Body to 2nd marked st, sc in marked st, sc 15 around 2nd Arm, sc in remaining Body sts—84 sc.
Rnds 9–11: Sc around.
Rnd 12: [Sc 6, invdec, sc 6] around—78 sc.
Rnd 13: [Invdec, sc 11] around—72 sc.
Rnd 14: [Sc 5, invdec, sc 5] around—66 sc.
Rnd 15: [Invdec, sc 9] around—60 sc.
Rnd 16: [Sc 4, invdec, sc 4] around—54 sc.
Rnd 17: [Invdec, sc 7] around—48 sc.
Rnd 18: [Sc 3, invdec, sc 3] around—42 sc.
Rnd 19: [Invdec, sc 5] around—36 sc.
Rnd 20: [Sc 2, invdec, sc 2] around—30 sc.
Fasten off. Stuff Body firmly.

Bottom of Robes

With **C** join to any unworked FL on Rnd 9 of Lower Body.
Rnd 1: Ch 1, sc in unworked FLO around, join—54 sc.
Rnd 2: Ch 1, [sc 4, inc, sc 4] around, join—60 sc.
Rnd 3: Ch 1, [inc, sc 9] around, join—66 sc.
Fasten off.

Robe Swirls (Make 8)

With **C**.
Row 1: Ch 12, 2 dc in 3rd ch from the hook, 3 dc in next 5 chs, dc 3, 3 dc in last ch, rotate to work in underside of starting ch, dc 3, ch 8, 2 dc in 3rd ch from hook, 3 dc in

next 4 chs, (3 dc, sl st) in last ch—43 sts.

Fasten off, leaving a long tail for sewing. Sew Swirls to bottom of Robes spaced evenly around. Weave in ends.

Outer Robe

With **C**.

Row 1: Ch 62, hdc in 3rd ch from hook (skipped chs do not count as a st), hdc in each ch across, turn—60 hdc.

Rows 2–22: Ch 1, hdc across, turn.

Fasten off, leaving a long tail for sewing. Wrap piece widthwise around Lower Body and sew 2 corners to right shoulder of Upper Body. Weave in ends.

Chin

With **A** make a magic ring.

Rnd 1: 6 sc in ring—6 sc.

Rnd 2: Inc around—12 sc.

Rnds 3–4: Sc around.

Fasten off. Stuff. Set Chin aside to join to Head.

Head

With **A** join to back of Upper Body in BL of st.

Rnd 1: Ch 1, working in BLO sc around, join—30 sc.

Rnd 2: Ch 1 tightly, [sc 4, invdec, sc 4] around, do not join—27 sc.

Rnd 3: [Invdec, sc 7] around—24 sc.

Rnd 4: [Sc 3, invdec, sc 3] around—21 sc.

Rnd 5: [Invdec, sc 5] around—18 sc.

Rnds 6–7: Sc around.

Using st markers mark 1 st at front center of Head where Chin will be joined. Hold Chin in line with Head to join in next rnd.

Rnd 8: Sc around to marked st, sc in marked st, sc 12 around Chin, sc in remaining sts of Head—30 sc.

Rnds 9–11: Sc around.

Rnd 12: [Inc, sc 9] around—33 sc.

Rnd 13: [Sc 5, inc, sc 5] around—36 sc.

Rnd 14: [Inc, sc 11] around—39 sc.

Rnd 15: [Sc 6, inc, sc 6] around—42 sc.

Rnds 16–26: Sc around.

Add eyes between Rnds 20 and 21, approximately 6 sts apart. Using a length of **A** held double, embroider nose between Rnds 16 and 17 over 3 sts. Using black embroidery thread, add under-eye details. Using **D** add eyebrows above eyes. Stuff Head and continue stuffing as work progresses.

Rnd 27: [Invdec, sc 5] around—36 sc.

Rnd 28: [Sc 2, invdec, sc 2] around—30 sc.

Rnd 29: [Invdec, sc 3] around—24 sc.

Rnd 30: [Sc, invdec, sc] around—18 sc.

Rnd 31: [Invdec, sc] around—12 sc.

Rnd 32: Invdec around—6 sc.

Fasten off, leaving a long tail for sewing. Sew remaining sts closed. Weave in ends.

Hair Crown

With **D** make a magic ring.

Rnd 1: 6 sc in ring.

Rnd 2: Inc around—12 sc.

Rnd 3: [Inc, sc] around—18 sc.

Rnd 4: [Sc, inc, sc] around—24 sc.

Rnd 5: [Inc, sc 3] around—30 sc.

Rnd 6: [Sc 2, inc, 2 sc] around—36 sc.

Rnd 7: [Inc, sc 5] around—42 sc.

Begin working in rows.

Row 8: Sc 28, turn leaving remaining sts unworked—28 sc.

Rows 9–16: Ch 1, sc across, turn.

Rows 17–19: Ch 1, sc2tog, sc across to last 2 sts, sc2tog, turn—22 sts at the end of Row 19.

Fasten off, leaving a long tail for sewing. Sew Hair Crown to top of Head. Weave in end.

Hair Strips (Make 4)

With **D**.

Row 1: Ch 5, sc in 2nd ch from hook, sc, hdc, dc, *ch 6, sc in 2nd ch from hook, sc, hdc, dc, skip last ch; repeat from * 4 more times—6 hair strands.

Fasten off **D**. With **E** join to underside of first ch with RS facing.

Row 2: Ch 1, *sc in next 4 chs, 3 sc in next, sc in next 4 sts, sl st in next ch; repeat across.

Fasten off leaving a long tail for sewing.

Hair Spikes (Make 9)

With **D**.

Row 1: Ch 9, sc in 2nd ch from hook, sc 6, 3 sc in last ch, rotate to work in underside of ch, sc 7—17 sc.

Fasten off. With **E** join to first sc of Row 1.

Row 2: Ch 1, sc 7, inc, (sc, ch 4, sc in 2nd ch from hook, sc in next 2 chs, sc) in next st, inc, sc 7—23 sc.

Finishing

Sew Hair Strip starting at front hairline and working backward to nape of neck, adding Hair Spikes between the strips to fill in the gaps. Weave in ends.

Jafar

Designed by Lee Sartori

Skill Level: Easy

Being a "right-hand man" has its perks, but there is something to say about professional advancement. Dream jobs are one in a million, and Jafar is *so close* to landing his. Sure, it's the position currently held by the ruling sultan of Agrabah, but why settle for being royal vizier when the throne is so close? There are just a few barriers in the way. Pesky ones like a poor street urchin named Aladdin who crosses paths with Jafar by chance during a heist gone sideways. Now the key to Jafar's ultimate goal—*power*—is a magic lamp containing an incredible genie capable of granting three wishes. Unfortunately, Aladdin has it . . . for now.

They say dress for the job you want, and in this pattern, Jafar is dressed to impress in his long, flowing robe! It's all in the details, so be sure to give your crocheted Jafar some menacing eyebrows. And don't forget his magical staff . . . It helps him get things done!

"A snake, am I? Perhaps you'd like to see how snakelike I can be."

—Jafar, *Aladdin* (1992)

YARN

Worsted weight (#4 medium) yarn, shown in Lion Brand Basic Stitch Anti Pilling™ (100% acrylic, 185 yd. / 170 m per 3.5 oz. / 100 g skein)

Color A: #122T Hazelnut, 1 skein

Color B: #153 Black, 1 skein

Color C: #400G Red Heather, 1 skein

Color D: #158L Mustard, 1 skein

HOOK

US D (3.25 mm) crochet hook

NOTIONS

Pair of 9 mm black safety eyes
Bamboo rod, 4 mm diameter
Stitch markers
Polyester stuffing
Yarn needle
Scissors

FINISHED MEASUREMENTS

Height: 14" / 35 cm
Width: 6" / 15 cm

SPECIAL STITCHES

Inc (increase) = Work 2 sc in the next st.

Invdec (invisible single crochet decrease) = Insert hook in front loop only of each of next 2 sts, yo and draw through both sts, yo and draw through 2 loops on hook—1 st decreased.

Popcorn (popcorn stitch) = Work 5 dc in next st, drop loop on hook, insert hook from front to back in first dc made, place dropped loop on hook and draw through dc.

Picot = Ch 3, sl st in 3rd ch from hook.

NOTES

- Work in continuous rounds unless otherwise indicated.
- When indicated, join at the end of a round with a slip stitch in the first stitch. To join new yarn to a stitch, insert hook in stitch and pull up a loop in indicated color.
- To change colors, work the last yarn over of the previous stitch with the new color. Fasten off previous color unless otherwise indicated.
- If desired, instead of making a magic ring, chain 2 and work indicated stitches in the 2nd chain from the hook.

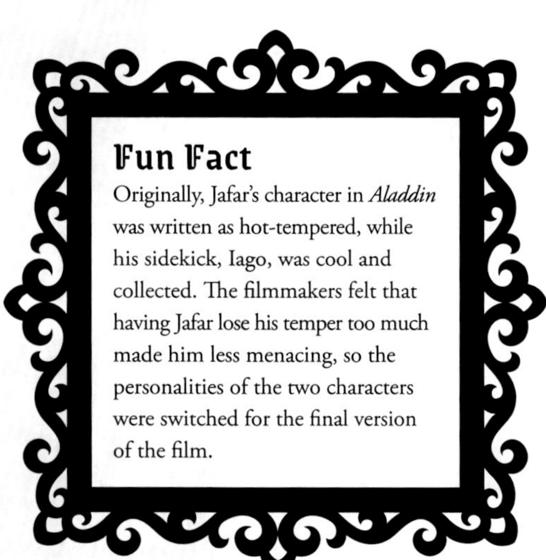

Fun Fact

Originally, Jafar's character in *Aladdin* was written as hot-tempered, while his sidekick, Iago, was cool and collected. The filmmakers felt that having Jafar lose his temper too much made him less menacing, so the personalities of the two characters were switched for the final version of the film.

Arms (Make 2)

With **A**, make a magic ring.
Rnd 1: 6 sc in ring—6 sc.
Rnd 2: Inc around—12 sc.
Rnds 3–4: Sc around.
Rnd 5: Popcorn, sc 11.
Rnds 6–7: Sc around.
Rnd 8: Invdec around—6 sc.
Change to **B**.
Rnd 9: Working in BLO, ch 1, sc around, join.
Rnds 10–13: Sc around.
Change to **C**.
Rnd 14: Working in FLO, 3 sc in each st around, join—18 sc.
Rnd 15: Ch 1 tightly, working in BLO sc around, do not join.
Rnds 16–17: Sc around.
Rnd 18: [Sc 2, invdec, sc 2] around—15 sc.
Rnds 19–20: Sc around.
Rnd 21: [Invdec, sc 3] around—12 sc.
Rnds 22–23: Sc around.
Fasten off. Set aside to join to Body.

Body

With **B** make a magic ring.
Rnd 1: 6 sc in ring—6 sc.
Rnd 2: Inc around—12 sc.
Rnd 3: [Inc, sc] around—18 sc.
Rnd 4: [Sc, inc, sc] around—24 sc.
Rnd 5: [Inc, sc 3] around—30 sc.
Rnd 6: [Sc 2, inc, 2 sc] around—36 sc.
Rnd 7: [Inc, sc 5] around—42 sc.
Rnd 8: [Sc 3, inc, sc 3] around—48 sc.
Rnd 9: [Inc, sc 7] around—54 sc.
Rnd 10: Working in BLO [sc 4, inc, sc 4] around—60 sc.
Rnds 11–12: Sc around.
Rnd 13: [Sc 9, invdec, sc 9] around—57 sc.
Rnd 14: Sc around.
Rnd 15: [Invdec, sc 17] around—54 sc.
Rnd 16: Sc around.
Rnd 17: [Sc 8, invdec, sc 8] around—51 sc.
Rnd 18: Sc around.
Rnd 19: [Invdec, sc 15] around—48 sc.
Rnd 20: Sc around.
Rnd 21: [Sc 7, invdec, sc 7]—45 sc.
Rnd 22: Sc around.
Rnd 23: [Invdec, sc 13] around—42 sc.
Rnd 24: Sc around.
Rnd 25: [Sc 6, invdec, sc 6] around—39 sc.
Rnd 26: Sc around.
Rnd 27: [Invdec, sc 11] around—36 sc.
Rnds 28–37: Sc around.
Change to **C**.
Rnd 38: Ch 1, working in BLO, sc around, join.
Rnds 39–40: Ch 1, sc around, join.
Change to **B**.
Rnd 41: Ch 1, working in BLO, sc around, join.
Rnd 42: Ch 1 tightly, [inc, sc 11] around, do not join—39 sc.
Rnd 43: [Sc 6, inc, sc 6] around—42 sc.
Rnd 44: [Inc, sc 13] around—45 sc.
Rnd 45: [Sc 7, inc, sc 7] around—48 sc.
Rnd 46: [Inc, sc 15] around—51 sc.
Rnd 47: [Sc 8, inc, sc 8] around—54 sc.

Using st markers, mark 1 sc on either side of Body where Arm will be joined, with 26 sc between markers for front of Body, and 26 sc between markers for back of Body. Hold Arms in line with Body to join in next rnd.

Rnd 48: Sc around Body to first marked st, sc in marked st, sc 12 around Arm to join, sc around Body to 2nd marked st, sc in marked st, sc 12 around 2nd Arm to join, sc in remaining sts on Body—78 sc.

Rnds 49–52: Sc around.

Rnd 53: [Invdec, sc 11] around—72 sc.

Rnd 54: [Sc 5, invdec, sc 5] around—66 sc.

Rnd 55: [invdec, sc 9] around—60 sc.

Rnd 56: [Sc 4, invdec, sc 4] around—54 sc.

Rnd 57: [Invdec, sc 7] around—48 sc.

Rnd 58: [Sc 3, invdec, sc 3] around—42 sc.

Rnd 59: [Invdec, sc 5] around—36 sc.

Rnd 60: [Sc 2, invdec, sc 2] around—30 sc.

Fasten off. Stuff Body. Using a length of **C**, embroider a vertical line from final row of Body to center of Body, and from center of Body to midway down skirt, using photos as a guide. Weave in ends.

Chin

With **A** make a magic ring.

Rnd 1: 6 sc in ring—6 sc.

Rnd 2: Sc around.

Fasten off. Set aside to join to Head.

Neck

With **D** join to sc on back of Body in BL.

Rnd 1: Ch 1, working in BLO sc around, join—30 sc.

Rnd 2: [Sc 4, invdec, sc 4] around—27 sc.

Rnd 3: [Invdec, sc 7] around—24 sc.

Rnd 4: [Sc 3, invdec, sc 3] around—21 sc.

Rnd 5: [Invdec, sc 5] around—18 sc.

Rnd 6: Inc around, join—36 sc.

Fasten off, continue to Head.

Head

Join **A** in sc on back of Neck.

Rnd 1: Ch 1, [inc, sc 5] around—42 sc.

Use st marker to mark middle front st where Chin will be joined. Hold Chin in line with Head to join on next rnd.

Rnd 2: Ch 1, sc around to marked st, sc in marked st, sc 6 around chin to join, sc in remaining sts on Head—48 sc.

Rnds 3–14: Sc around.

Fasten off **A**. Add safety eyes between Rnds 11 and 12 approximately 6 sts apart. Using a length of **A** held double embroider Nose between Rnds 9 and 10 over 3 sts. Using a length of **B** add eyebrows above eyes and a mustache below nose using photo as a guide.

Goatee

With **B**.

Row 1: Ch 10 tightly.

Fasten off leaving a long tail for sewing. Sew to bottom of Chin. Weave in ends.

Headscarf

WIth **C** leaving a long tail at start for sewing.

Row 1: Ch 31, starting in 2nd ch from hook sc across, turn—30 sc.

Rows 2–17: Ch 1, sc across, turn.

Fasten off. Weave in end. Using starting tail, sew scarf to back 30 sc of Head in FLO. Weave in ends.

Turban

With **B** make a magic ring.
Rnd 1: 6 sc in ring—6 sc.
Rnd 2: Inc around—12 sc.
Rnd 3: [Inc, sc] around—18 sc.
Rnd 4: Inc 6, sc 12—24 sc.
Rnd 5: [Inc, sc] 6 times, sc 12—30 sc.
Rnd 6: [Sc, inc, sc] 6 times, sc 12—36 sc.
Rnd 7: [Inc, sc 3] 6 times, sc 12—42 sc.
Rnd 8: [Sc 2, inc, sc 2] 6 times, sc 12—48 sc.
Rnds 9–18: Sc around.
Fasten off leaving a long tail for sewing.

Jewel

With **C** make a magic ring.
Rnd 1: 6 sc in ring, join—6 sc.
Change to **D**.
Rnd 2: Ch 1, sl st around, join.
Fasten off leaving a long tail for sewing.

Feather

With **C**.
Row 1: Ch 15, starting in 2nd ch from hook, sl st 5, sc 8, (sc 2, picot, sc 2) in last ch, rotate to work in underside of starting ch, sc 8, sl st 5—20 sc.
Fasten off leaving a long tail for sewing. Sew to front of Turban with picot stitch at the top. Weave in ends. Sew the Jewel to the bottom of the Feather.

Gold Detail

With **D**.

Row 1: Ch 50 tightly.

Fasten off. Sew Gold Detail around Turban using photos as a guide. Weave in ends.

Lower Robes

Join **B** to back of Body in unworked FL of Rnd 9.

Rnd 1: Ch 1, working in unworked FLO, [sc 4, inc, sc 4] around—60 sc.

Rnd 2: Ch 1, [inc, sc 9] around, join—66 sc.

Fasten off. Weave in ends.

Shoulder Pads (Make 2 with C and 2 with B)

Make a magic ring.

Rnd 1: 6 sc in ring—6 sc.

Rnd 2: Inc around—12 sc.

Rnd 3: [Inc, sc] around—18 sc.

Rnd 4: [Sc, inc, sc] around—24 sc.

Rnd 5: [Inc, sc 3] around—30 sc.

Fasten off **C**. Do not fasten off **B**. Place one **C** pad and one **B** pad together to join in next rnd.

Rnd 6: With **B**, ch 1, working through both thicknesses, sc around, join—30 sc.

Fasten off, leaving a long tail for sewing. Sew Shoulder Pad to top of each shoulder. Weave in ends.

Cape (Make 1 with C and 1 with B)

Row 1: Ch 36, starting in 2nd ch from hook sc across, turn—35 sc.

Rows 2–51: Ch 1, sc across, turn.

Fasten off **C**. Do not fasten off **B**. Place Capes together to join in next Rnd.

Rnd 52: With **B**, ch 1, working through both thicknesses, sc in each row end and st around, making a ch 2 in each corner, join.

Fasten off, leaving a long tail for sewing. Sew Cape to back of Body with **C** facing inside of Body and **B** facing out.

Staff

With **D** make a magic ring.

Rnd 1: 6 sc in ring—6 sc.

Rnd 2: Inc around—12 sc.

Rnds 3–4: Sc around.

Rnd 5: [Invdec, sc] around—8 sc.

Stuff.

Rnd 6: [Invdec, sc 2] around—6 sc.

Rnds 7–56: Sc around.

Insert bamboo rod into Staff. Fasten off leaving a long tail. Sew remaining 6 sts closed in BLO. Weave in ends.

Staff Sides (Make 2)

With **D**.

Row 1: Ch 2, 3 sc in 2nd ch from hook, turn—3 sc.

Row 2: Ch 1, inc across, turn—6 sc.

Row 3: Ch 1, [inc, sc] across, turn—9 sc.

Rows 4–5: Ch 1, sc across, turn.

Fasten off leaving a long tail for sewing. Sew to sides of Staff using photos as a guide.

Staff Nose

With **D** make a magic ring.

Rnd 1: 4 sc in ring, join—4 sc.

Fasten off leaving a long tail for sewing. Sew to front of Staff. Using **C** add eye details above Nose.

Doctor Facilier

Designed by Nicole Rogowski

Skill Level: Advanced

Doctor Facilier is a man on a mission, and that mission is to control New Orleans. Facilier may already be known around town, feared even. But he's after a different kind of power: wealth. So, when he learns that the penniless Prince Naveen has come to stay with "Big Daddy" La Bouff, Facilier hatches a plan. Realizing that La Bouff hopes the prince will fall in love with his daughter, Charlotte, Facilier conspires to transform the prince into a frog. As part of this nefarious plot, Facilier intends to have Naveen's butler, Lawrence, turned into a physical replica of the prince. The two agree that if Charlotte weds Lawrence, they'll split her La Bouff inheritance. Some in town might say it's a plan resting on parlor tricks, but it sure seems to be working. At least, until the real Prince Naveen meets Charlotte's best friend, Tiana. She kisses the prince in hopes of breaking the spell, just like in the fairy tale her mother used to tell about a Frog Prince. Only . . . Tiana is transformed into a frog herself. Now, if this were a game of chance, the odds might be tipping in Doctor Facilier's favor.

A stylish top hat, a suave suit, and a winning attitude make Doctor Facilier an *awfully* charming Disney Villain. If what you want is a cute amigurumi version of him, this crochet pattern has the power to give it to you. And unlike Doctor Facilier's deals, this one isn't likely to cost you what you already have.

"No! I'm not ready at all! In fact, I got lots more plans! This is just a minor setback in a major operation."

—Doctor Facilier, *The Princess and the Frog* (2009)

YARN

Worsted weight (#4 medium) yarn, shown in Lion Brand Basic Stitch Anti Pilling™ (100% acrylic, 185 yd. / 170 m per 3.5 oz. / 100 g skein)

Color A: #124AD Nutmeg, 1 skein
Color B: #138L Pomegranate, 1 skein
Color C: #100 White, 1 skein
Color D: #400G Red Heather, 1 skein
Color E: #112S Deco Rose, 1 skein
Color F: #153 Black, 1 skein

HOOK

US F (3.75 mm) crochet hook

NOTIONS

Pair of 5 mm safety eyes
Stitch markers
Polyester stuffing
Yarn needle
Scissors

FINISHED MEASUREMENTS

Height: 15" / 37.5 cm
Width: 3.5" / 9 cm

SPECIAL STITCHES

Inc (increase) = Work 2 sc in next st.

Invdec (invisible single crochet decrease) = Insert hook in front loop only of each of next 2 sts, yo and draw through both sts, yo and draw through 2 loops on hook—1 st decreased.

Exsc (extended single crochet) = Insert hook into indicated st, yo and draw up a loop, yo and draw through 1 loop, yo and draw through 2 loops. *Note: Make your next sc tightly to secure this stitch.

Bpexsc (back post extended single crochet) = Insert hook from back to front to back again around post of next st, yo and draw up a loop, yo and draw through 1 loop, yo and draw through 2 loops.

Bpsc (back post single crochet) = Insert hook from back to front to back again around post of next st, yo and draw up a loop, yo and draw through 2 loops.

Bpsc2tog (back post single crochet 2 together) = [Insert hook from back to front to back again around post of next st, yo and draw up a loop] twice, yo and draw through all loops on hook—1 st decreased.

Sc2tog (single crochet 2 together) = [Insert hook in next st, yo and draw up a loop] twice, yo and draw through all loops on hook—1 st decreased.

Sc3tog (single crochet 3 stitches together) = [Insert hook into next st, yo and draw up a loop] 3 times, yo and draw through all loops on hook—2 sts decreased.

Bobble (bobble stitch) = [Yo, insert hook into st, yo and draw up a loop, yo and draw through 2 loops on hook] 3 times, yo and draw through all loops on hook.

Brm (Brim Stitch) = Yo, insert hook in st, yo and draw up a loop, yo and draw through 1 loop on hook, [yo and draw through 2 loops on hook] twice (extended dc made), yo, hook between bottom legs of extended dc just made, yo and draw up a loop, [yo and draw through 2 loops on hook] twice (2nd dc made).

Exdc (extended double crochet) = Yo and insert hook into indicated st, yo and draw up a loop, yo and draw through 1 loop, [yo and draw through 2 loops] twice.

GAUGE

20 sc and 22 rnds = 4 in. / 10 cm in sc

Gauge is not critical for this project. Ensure your stitches are tight so the stuffing won't show through.

NOTES

- Work in continuous rounds unless otherwise indicated.
- When indicated, join at the end of a round with a slip stitch in the first stitch. To join new yarn to a stitch, insert hook in stitch and pull up a loop in indicated color.
- To change colors, work the last yarn over of the previous stitch with the new color. Fasten off previous color unless otherwise indicated.
- If desired, instead of making a magic ring, chain 2 and work indicated stitches in the 2nd chain from the hook.

Arms (Make 2)

With **A**, ch 9, being careful not to twist, sl st in first ch to form a ring.

Rnd 1: Ch 1, sc in each ch around—9 sc.

Rnd 2: [Sc, invdec] twice, sc 3—7 sc.

Rnds 3–8: Sc around.

Rnd 9: [Sc, invdec] twice, sc—5 sc.

Rnd 10: Sc around.

Rnd 11: Sc 2, inc, sc 2—6 sc.

Rnds 12–16: Sc around.

Rnd 17: [Invdec] 3 times—3 sc.

Rnd 18: Working in FLO, inc around—6 sc.

Rnd 19: Sc around, ch 4, starting in 2nd ch from hook, sc 2, sl st (*thumb made*)—6 sc, 3-st thumb.

On next rnd, skip all thumb sts and make sure thumb stays to outside of hand.

Rnds 20–24: Sc around—6 sc.

Fasten off leaving a long tail for sewing. Sew remaining 6 sts closed. Weave in ends.

Legs (Make 2)

With **B** make a magic ring.

Rnd 1: Ch 1, 5 sc in ring—5 sts.

Rnd 2: Sc around.

Rnd 3: Inc, sc 4—6 sts.

Change to **C**.

Rnd 4: Working in FLO, [sc, inc] 3 times—9 sts.

Rnd 5: Sc around.

Rnd 6: Sc 6, with **B**, sc 3, join, turn.

Begin working in turned rows for the heel of the foot. Continue with **B**.

Heel Row 1 (WS): Ch 1, sc 2, sl st, turn leaving remaining sts unworked—2 sc.

Heel Row 2 (RS): Ch 1, sc 2, sc in ch-1 from Row 1, sl st in next unworked st of Rnd 6, turn—3 sc.

Heel Row 3: Ch 1, sc 3, sc in ch-1 from Row 2, sl st in next unworked st of Rnd 6, turn—4 sc.

Resume working in rounds.

Change to **C**.

Rnd 7: Ch 1, working in FLO, exsc 4, sc2tog in ch-1 from Heel Row 3 and next unworked st from Rnd 6, sc, sc2tog in next unworked st from Rnd 6 and beginning ch-1 of current rnd—7 sts.

Rnd 8: Exsc around.

Rnd 9: Sc around, join.

Change to **B**.

Rnd 10: Ch 2 (*does not count as st here and throughout*), working in FLO, 2 dc in each st around, join—14 sts.

Rnd 11: Ch 1, bpexsc around.

Rnds 12–13: Sc around.

Rnd 14: [Sc, invdec] 4 times, sc 2—10 sc.

Rnds 15–18: Sc around.

Rnd 19: [Sc 3, invdec] twice—8 sc.

Rnds 20–35: Sc around.

Rnd 36: [Sc, inc] twice, sc 4—10 sc.

Rnds 37–38: Sc around.

Fasten off first Leg. Do not fasten off 2nd Leg.

Holding Legs together, with toes pointed in same direction, seam first 3 sts of inner thigh of both Legs together with sl st. Sl st in next st of 2nd Leg for new beginning of round. Continue to Body.

Body

Skip seamed sts of inner thigh on next rnd.

Rnd 1: Ch 1, [sc 6, inc] around 2nd Leg, [sc 6, inc] around first Leg—16 sts.

Rnds 2–3: Sc around.

Sc 8, join in next st to shift beginning of rnd on back of Body in line with split of Legs.

Change to **D**.

Rnd 4: Ch 1, working in BLO, sc around.

Rnds 5–6: Sc around. At end of last rnd, join.

Change to **A**.

Rnd 7: Working in BLO, sl st around.

Rnd 8: Working in BLO, sc around.

Rnd 9: Sc around, join.

Change to **E**.

Rnd 10: Working in BLO, sl st around.

Rnd 11: Ch 1, working in BLO, sc around.

Rnds 12–13: Sc around.

Rnd 14: [Sc 3, inc] 4 times—20 sc.

Rnd 15: Sc around.

Rnd 16: [Sc 4, inc] 4 times—24 sc.

Rnd 17: Sc 6, inc, sc 15, inc, sc—26 sc.

Rnd 18: Sc 8, inc 2, sc 11, inc 2, sc 3—30 sc.

In underside of foundation chs of Arm, mark 4 sts on each Arm at underarm to begin joining to Body in next rnd. Begin working with 2 colors each rnd. Do not fasten off until indicated.

Rnd 19: With **E** sc 7 on Body, with **A** sc, working through both thicknesses sc 4 through both Body and marked sts on first Arm, continuing on Body only sc, with **E** sc 9, with **A** sc, working through both thicknesses sc 4 through both Body and marked sts on 2nd Arm, continuing on Body only sc, with **E** sc 2.

On next rnd work on Body and remaining unworked underside of foundation chs of Arms as directed to complete joining. Skip all sc used to join Arms in previous rnd.

Rnd 20: Continue on Body with **E** sc 7, with **A** sc, inc 5 around unworked Arm sts, continuing on Body sc, with **E** sc 9, with **A** sc, inc 5 around unworked sts on next Arm, continuing on Body sc, with **E** sc 2—42 sc.

Rnd 21: With **E** sc 7, with **A** sc 12, with **E** sc 9, with **A** sc 12, with **E** sc 2.

Rnd 22: With **E** sc 8, with **A** [sc 2, invdec] twice, sc 2, with **E** sc 11, with **A** [sc 2, invdec] twice, sc 2, with **E** sc 3—38 sc.

Rnd 23: With **E** sc 8, with **A** sc, [sc3tog] twice, sc, with **E** sc 11, with **A** sc, [sc3tog] twice, sc, with **E** sc 3, join—30 sc.

Rnd 24: With **A** sc 6, with **E** sc 2, [invdec] twice, sc 2, with **A** sc 7, with **E** sc 2, [invdec] twice, sc 2, with **A** sc—26 sts.

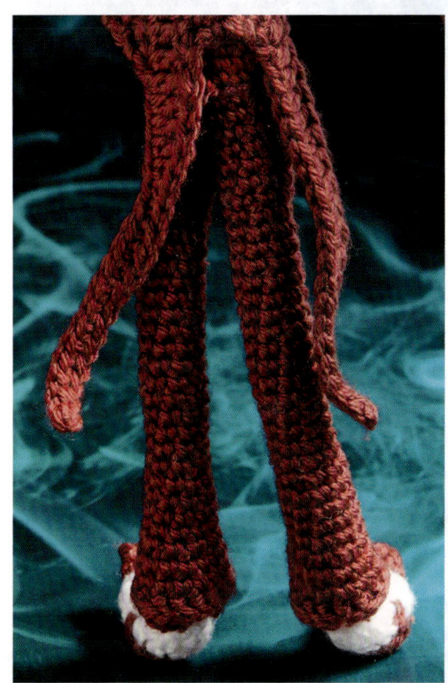

Rnd 25: With **A** [invdec, sc] twice, with **E** [invdec] 3 times, with **A** [sc, invdec] twice, sc, with **E** [invdec] 3 times, with **A** sc—16 sts.

Fasten off **E**. Continue with **A**.

Rnd 26: Sc, invdec, sc, sc3tog, sc, invdec, sc 2, sc3tog, sc—10 sc.

Continue to Head.

Head

With **A**.

Rnds 1–2: Sc around—10 sc.

Rnd 3: Sc 6, working in FLO, sc, hdc 2, sc.

Rnd 4: Inc 7, [2 hdc in next st] twice, inc—20 sts.

Begin working with 2 colors per rnd. Do not fasten off until indicated.

Rnd 5: With **A** sc 2, with **F** [sc 2, inc] twice, with **A** sc 6, hdc, [2 hdc in next st] twice, hdc, sc 2—24 sts.

Rnd 6: With **A** sc 2, with **F** sc, invdec, sc 4, invdec, with **A** sc 5, [invdec] 3 times, sc 2—19 sts.

Rnd 7: With **A** sc 2, with **F** sc, invdec, sc 2, invdec, sc, with **A** sc 3, [invdec, sc] twice—15 sts.

Rnd 8: With **A** sc 2, with **F** sc 6, with **A** sc 4, inc, sc 2—16 sc.

Rnd 9: With **A** sc 2, with **F** sc, inc, sc 2, inc, sc, with **A** sc 5, bobble, sc 2—18 sts.

Rnd 10: With **A** sc 2, with **F** sc 8, with **A** sc 5, fpsc, sc 2.

Rnds 11–12: With **A** sc 2, with **F** sc 8, with **A** sc 8. At the end of Rnd 12, join.

Change to **F**.

Place the safety eyes (if using), between the 14th and 15th sts and 17th and 18th sts from Rnd 10.

On the next rnd, work around the posts of sts leaving the top loops unworked for the body of the Hat.

Rnd 13: Ch 2 (*does not count as st here and throughout*), turn, Brm around, join. Fasten off—36 sts.

Continue to Hat.

Hat

Join **D** to the 9th st of Rnd 12 of Head.

Rnd 1: Ch 1, sc around—18 sc.

Rnds 2–3: Sc around. At the end of Rnd 3, join.

Change to **F**.

Rnd 4: Working in BLO, sl st around.

Rnd 5: Working in BLO, sc around.

Rnds 6–10: Sc around.

Rnd 11: [Sc 2, inc] 6 times—24 sc.

Rnds 12–13: Sc around. At the end of Rnd 13, join.

Rnd 14: Ch 1, [bpsc, bpsc2tog] 8 times—16 sc.

Rnd 15: Invdec around—8 sc.

Rnd 16: Sc around, join.

Fasten off leaving a long tail. Use tail to sew remaining sts closed.

Skull and Crossbones

With **C**, make a magic ring leaving a 20" tail.

Rnd 1: Ch 1, 8 sc in ring, join—8 sc.

Fasten off leaving a 16" long tail.

If needed, split yarn into individual plies for embroidering.

Use 20" tail to sew circle on center front of Hat. With 16" tail, embroider 2 small vertical stitches for teeth, large X for crossbones, and short Vs to create the knobby ends of the bones.

Use photos as a guide. With **F**, embroider Skull nose and French knot eyes.

Fang Necklace

If needed, split yarn into individual plies for embroidering.

With **C**, embroider 2 long fangs (2 rnds tall) 3 sts apart on front of neckline. With **F**, embroider the necklace around, working through the strands of the embroidered fangs.

Left Ear

With **A**.

Row 1: Ch 3, starting in 2nd ch from hook, inc, [2 hdc, ch 1, sl st] in last ch—4 sts.

Fasten off leaving long tail for sewing. Sew to Head, 4 sts away from the nose.

Right Ear

With **A**.

Row 1: Ch 3, starting in 2nd ch from hook, 2 hdc in first ch, [inc, ch 1, sl st] in last ch—4 sts.

Fasten off leaving long tail for sewing. Sew to Head, 4 sts away from the nose.

Jacket

Before continuing, weave in all ends on Body.

With **B**.

Row 1: Ch 15, starting in 2nd ch from hook, working into back bumps of chs, sc across, turn—14 sc.

Row 2: Ch 1, inc, sc 13, turn—15 sc.

Row 3: Ch 1, sc 14, inc, ch 19, turn—16 sc, 19 chs.

Row 4: Starting in 2nd ch from hook, working into back bumps of chs, sl st 2, sc 6, exsc 6, exdc 4, continuing *across previous row,* exdc 8, ch 7, skip 7 (armhole made), exdc, turn—27 sts including sl sts, 7 chs.

Row 5: Ch 2 (*does not count as st here and throughout*), exdc, exdc in each ch across, exdc, exsc, sc 4, invdec, turn leaving remaining sts unworked—15 sts.

Row 6: Ch 1, invdec, sc 3, exsc, exdc 9, turn—14 sts.

Row 7: Ch 2, exdc 9, exsc, sc 3, sl st, turn.

Row 8: Ch 1, inc in sl st, sc 3, exsc, exdc 9, turn—15 sts.

Row 9: Ch 2, exdc, ch 7, skip 7 (armhole made), exdc, exsc, sc 4, inc, ch 19, turn—9 sts, 1 ch-7, 1 ch-19.

Row 10: Starting in 2nd ch from hook, working into back bumps of chs, sl st 2, sc 6, exsc 6, exdc 4, *continuing across previous row,* invdec, sc 6, sc in each ch, sc, turn—33 sts including sl sts.

Row 11: Sc 13, invdec, turn leaving remaining sts unworked—14 sts.

Row 12: Sc across, rotate to work across row ends, ch 1, evenly work 16 sc across row ends, ch 1, join to underside of foundation ch.

Fasten off leaving a 16" long tail.

Jacket Sleeves (Make 2)

With **B**. Join to first skipped st of armhole.

Rnd 1: Ch 1, exsc in each skipped st, exsc 2 across armhole corner, exsc in underside of chs, exsc 2 across last armhole corner—18 sts.

Rnd 2: Working in FLO, [sc, invdec] around—12 sc.

Rnds 3–11: Exsc around.

Rnd 12: [Exdc 5, 2 exdc in next] twice, join—14 sts.

Fasten off.

Repeat for 2nd armhole.

Jacket Collar

With **F** join with sl st to 6th st of Row 12 of Jacket.

Row 1: Working in BLO, skip same st as join, sl st 8, skip corner ch-1, sl st 16 across top of Jacket, skip corner ch-1, working in underside of foundation chs sl st 9, turn leaving remaining sts unworked—34 sts.

Row 2: Ch 1, working in BLO, sl st 3, sc, exsc, (exdc, ch 1, picot, ch 2, sl st) in next st, (sl st, ch 2, exdc) in next st, exdc, exsc 18, exdc, (edc, ch 2, sl st) in next st, (sl st, ch 3, sl in 2nd ch from hook, exdc) in next st, exsc, sc, sl st 3.

Fasten off.

Weave in all short ends, place Jacket on Body, and use 16" tail to tack in place.

✦✦✦✦✦✦✦✦

"Got to hand it to you, Tiana. When you dream, you dream big."

—Doctor Facilier, *The Princess and the Frog* (2009)

Maleficent

Designed by Lee Sartori

Skill Level: Intermediate

It's time to celebrate! The beautiful baby Princess Aurora has been born to the King and Queen and the entire kingdom is ready to share in their joy. Special guests include three good fairies, Flora, Fauna, and Merryweather, who are set to bestow magical gifts to the much-anticipated new arrival. The festivities are joyous until an uninvited guest appears . . . the evil fairy Maleficent. Feeling slighted at the exclusion from such an important event, Maleficent curses the young princess, announcing to all that Aurora will prick her finger on a spinning wheel's spindle and die before sunset on her sixteenth birthday. As the story unfolds, it seems safe to say that the King and Queen will rue the day they aggrieved Maleficent.

What's the etiquette for an old friend who didn't receive a party invite? Released in 1959, *Sleeping Beauty* is the Disney classic responsible for introducing fans to Maleficent, who has had one of the longest reigns as a Disney Villain. She's a pro! Crochet this powerful fairy in all of her fury and think of Maleficent the next time you create the guest list for your own celebrations!

"A forest of thorns shall be his tomb. Borne through the skies on a fog of doom! Now go with the curse and serve me well! Around Stefan's castle, cast my spell!"

—Maleficent, *Sleeping Beauty* (1959)

YARN

Worsted weight (#4 medium) yarn, shown in:

Yarn Citizen Unity Worsted (100% wool, 211 yd. / 193 m per 3.5 oz. / 100 g skein)

Color A: Sage, 1 skein

Lion Brand Basic Stitch Anti Pilling™ (100% acrylic, 185 yd. / 170 m per 3.5 oz. / 100 g skein)

Color B: #153 Black, 2 skeins

Color C: #112S Deco Rose, 1 skein

Lion Brand DIYarn (100% acrylic, 65 yd. / 60 m per 1.05 oz. / 30 g skein)

Color D: #195 Hot Pink, 1 skein

HOOK

US D (3.25 mm) crochet hook

NOTIONS

Pair of 12 mm black safety eyes

Stitch markers

Polyester stuffing

Yarn needle

Scissors

FINISHED MEASUREMENTS

Height: 13" / 32.5 cm

Width: 7" / 17.5 cm

SPECIAL STITCHES

Inc (increase) = Work 2 sc in next st.

Invdec (invisible single crochet decrease) = Insert hook in front loop only of each of next 2 sts, yo and draw through both sts, yo and draw through 2 loops on hook—1 st decreased.

Sc2tog (single crochet 2 together) = [Insert hook in next st, yo and draw up a loop] twice, yo and draw through all loops on hook—1 st decreased.

Picot = Ch 3, sl st in 3rd ch from hook.

Popcorn (popcorn stitch) = Work 5 dc in next st, drop loop on hook, insert hook from front to back in first dc of 5, place dropped loop on hook and draw it through the back of the first dc.

GAUGE
28 sc and 28 rnds = 4 in. / 10 cm in sc
Gauge is not critical for this project. Ensure your stitches are tight so the stuffing won't show through.

NOTES
- Work in continuous rounds unless otherwise indicated.
- When indicated, join at the end of a round with a slip stitch in the first stitch. To join new yarn to a stitch, insert hook in stitch and pull up a loop in indicated color.
- To change colors, work the last yarn over of the previous stitch with the new color. Fasten off previous color unless otherwise indicated.
- If desired, instead of making a magic ring, chain 2 and work indicated stitches in the 2nd chain from the hook.

Fun Fact

Eleanor Audley, the voice of Maleficent, was also one of the live-action models that the animators used for reference in drawing her dark fairy character.

"I really felt quite distressed at not receiving an invitation."

—Maleficent, *Sleeping Beauty* (1959)

Arms (Make 2)

With **A**, make a magic ring.
Rnd 1: 6 sc in ring—6 sc.
Rnd 2: Inc around—12 sc.
Rnds 3–4: Sc around.
Rnd 5: Popcorn, sc 11.
Rnds 6–7: Sc around.
Rnd 8: [Invdec, sc 2] around, join—9 sc.
Change to **B**.
Rnd 9: Ch 1, 3 sc in each sc around, join—27 sc.
Rnd 10: Ch 1, inc around, join—54 sc.
Rnd 11: Ch 1, sc around, join.
Rnd 12: Working in BLO, ch 1, sc and marked unworked FL left behind with a st marker, sc around, join.
Rnd 13: Ch 1, [invdec, sc 7] around, join—48 sc.
Rnd 14: Ch 1 tightly, [sc 7, invdec, sc 7] around, do not join—45 sc.
Rnd 15: [Invdec, sc 13] around—42 sc.
Rnd 16: [Sc 6, invdec, sc 6] around—39 sc.
Rnd 17: [Invdec, sc 11] around—36 sc.
Rnd 18: [Sc 5, invdec, sc 5] around—33 sc.
Rnd 19: [Invdec, sc 9] around—30 sc.
Rnd 20: [Sc 4, invdec, sc 4] around—27 sc.
Rnd 21: [Invdec, sc 7] around—24 sc.
Rnd 22: [Sc 3, invdec, sc 3] around—21 sc.
Rnd 23: [Invdec, sc 5] around—18 sc.
Rnd 24: [Sc 2, invdec, sc 2] around—15 sc.
Rnd 25: [Invdec, sc 3] around—12 sc.
Fasten off.
Join to marked st of Rnd 11 in FL.
Cuff Rnd 1: Ch 1, working in unworked FLO of each st of Rnd 11, sc around join—54 sc.
Change to **C**.
Cuff Rnd 2: Ch 1, [sc, picot, sc] around—54 sc, 27 picot.
Fasten off. Weave in ends. Stuff Arm lightly.

Body

With **B** make a magic ring.
Rnd 1: 6 sc in ring—6 sc.
Rnd 2: Inc around—12 sc.
Rnd 3: [Inc, sc] around—18 sc.
Rnd 4: [Sc, inc, sc] around—24 sc.
Rnd 5: [Inc, sc 3] around—30 sc.
Rnd 6: [Sc 2, inc, sc 2] around—36 sc.
Rnd 7: [Inc, sc 5] around—42 sc.
Rnd 8: [Sc 3, inc, sc 3] around—48 sc.
Rnd 9: [Inc, sc 7] around—54 sc.
Rnd 10: Working in BLO, [sc 4, inc, sc 4] around—60 sc.
Rnd 11: [Inc, sc 9] around—66 sc.
Rnd 12: [Sc 5, inc, sc 5] around, join—72 sc.
Rnd 13: Ch 1, working in BLO, sc in first st and mark unworked FL with a st marker, sc around, join.
Rnd 14: Ch 1 tightly, [sc 5, invdec, sc 5] around, do not join—66 sc.
Rnd 15: [Sc 10, invdec, sc 10] around—63 sc.
Rnd 16: [Invdec, sc 19] around—60 sc.
Rnd 17: [Sc 9, invdec, sc 9] around—57 sc.
Rnd 18: [Invdec, sc 17] around—54 sc.

Rnd 19: [Sc 8, invdec, sc 8] around—51 sc.
Rnd 20: [Invdec, sc 15] around—48 sc.
Rnd 21: [Sc 7, invdec, sc 7] around—45 sc.
Rnd 22: [Invdec, sc 13] around—42 sc.
Rnd 23: [Sc 6, invdec, sc 6] around—39 sc.
Rnd 24: [Invdec, sc 11] around—36 sc.
Rnds 25–44: Sc around.
Stuff and continue stuffing as work progresses.
Hold Arms in line with Body to join in next rnd.
Rnd 45: Sc 9, sc 12 around Arm to join, sc 18 on Body, sc 12 around next Arm to join, sc 9 on Body—60 sc.
Rnds 46–50: Sc around.
Rnd 51: [Sc 4, invdec, sc 4] around—54 sc.
Rnd 52: [Invdec, sc 7] around—48 sc.
Rnd 53: [Sc 3, invdec, sc 3] around—42 sc.
Rnd 54: [Invdec, sc 5] around—36 sc.
Rnd 55: [Sc 2, invdec, sc 2] around—30 sc.
Rnd 56: [Invdec, sc 3] around—24 sc.
Rnd 57: [Sc, invdec, sc] around—18 sc.
Fasten off. Stuff Body and tops of Arms.

Skirt

With **B** join in marked FL of Rnd 12 of Body.

Rnd 1: Ch 2 (*does not count as a st here and throughout*), dc in unworked FLO around, join—72 dc.

Rnd 2: Ch 2, [2 dc in next st, dc 11] around, join—78 dc.

Rnd 3: Ch 2, [dc 6, 2 dc in next st, dc 6] around, join—84 dc.

Rnd 4: Ch 2, [2 dc in next st, dc 13] around, join—90 dc.

Rnd 5: Ch 2, [dc 7, 2 dc in next st, dc 7] around, join—96 dc.

Change to **C**.

Rnd 6: Ch 1, [sc, picot, sc] around—96 sc, 48 picot.

Fasten off. Weave in ends.

Center Dress Detail

With **D**.

Row 1: Ch 19, starting in 2nd ch from hook, sl st 6, sc 6, hdc 6, turn—18 sts.

Row 2: Ch 2 (*does not count as a st*), working in BLO, hdc 6, sc 6, sl st 6, turn.

Row 3: Ch 1, working in BLO, sl st 6, sc 6, hdc 6, turn.

Change to **B**.

Row 4: Ch 1, working in BLO, sl st 18, ch 25, turn—18 sl st, 25 chs.

Row 5: Ch 1, sc in 2nd ch from hook, place st marker in underside of ch just worked in, sc in next 23 chs, working in BLO sc in next 18 sl st, turn—42 sts.

Row 6: Ch 1, sc across, turn—42 sc.

Change to **C** in FLO.

Row 7: Ch 1, working in FLO, sc across, turn.

Change to **B**.

Row 8: Ch 1, working in BLO, sc across, turn.

Row 9: Ch 1, sc across, turn.

Join with **D** in BLO.

Row 10: Ch 2, working in BLO, hdc 6, sc 6, sl st 6, turn leaving remaining sts unworked—18 sts.

Row 11: Ch 1, working in FLO, sl st 6, sc 6, hdc 6, turn.

Row 12: Ch 2, working in BLO hdc 6, sc 6, sl st 6, turn.

Row 13: Ch 1, working in FLO sl st 6, sc 6, hdc 6, turn.

Fasten off **D**, join with **B**.

Row 14: Ch 1, working in BLO, sc in next 18 sts, sc in 24 unworked sts of Row 9—42 sc.

Fasten off leaving a long tail for sewing.

With **B** join to marked ch at top of piece.

Edging: Ch 1, sc in underside of 24 chs of Row 4 and in underside of next 18 chs of Row 1—42 sc.

Fasten off leaving a long tail for sewing. Sew down the center of the Body from the neck to the hem. Weave in ends.

Head

With **A** join to back of Body in BL.

Rnd 1: Ch 1, working in BLO, sc around, join—18 sc.

Rnd 2: Ch 1, sc around, join.

Rnd 3: Ch 1 tightly, inc around, do not join—36 sc.

Rnd 4: [Inc, sc 5] around—42 sc.

Rnd 5: [Sc 3, inc, sc 3] around—48 sc.

Rnd 6: [Inc, sc 7] around—54 sc.

Rnds 7–20: Sc around.

Add safety eyes between Rnds 15 and 16 approximately 8 sts apart. Using a length of **B** and **C**, embroider eyebrows and makeup above eyes using photos as a guide. Using a length of **A** held double, embroider nose between Rnds 13 and 14 over 3 sts.

Rnd 21: [Invdec, sc 7] around—48 sc.

Rnd 22: [Sc 3, invdec, sc 3] around—42 sc.

Rnd 23: [Invdec, sc 5] around—36 sc.

Rnd 24: [Sc 2, invdec, sc 2] around—30 sc.

Stuff Head and continue stuffing as work progresses.

Rnd 25: [Invdec, sc 3] around—24 sc.

Rnd 26: [Sc, invdec, sc] around—18 sc.

Rnd 27: [Invdec, sc] around—12 sc.

Rnd 28: Invdec around—6 sc.

Fasten off leaving a long tail for sewing. Sew remaining 6 sts closed. Weave in end.

Head Piece

With **B** make a magic ring.

Rnd 1: 6 sc in ring—6 sc.

Rnd 2: Inc around—12 sc.

Rnd 3: [Inc, sc] around—18 sc.

Rnd 4: [Sc, inc, sc] around—24 sc.

Rnd 5: [Inc, sc 3] around—30 sc.

Rnd 6: [Sc 2, inc, sc 2] around—36 sc.

Rnd 7: [Inc, sc 5] around—42 sc.

Rnd 8: [Sc 3, inc, sc 3] around—48 sc.

Rnd 9: [Inc, sc 7] around—54 sc.

Rnds 10–14: Sc around.

Begin working in turned rows.

Row 15: Sc 8, turn leaving remaining sts unworked—8 sc.

Row 16: Ch 1, sc2tog, sc 4, sc2tog, turn—6 sc.

Row 17: Ch 1, sc2tog, sc 2, sc2tog, turn—4 sc.

Row 18: Ch 1, sc2tog twice, turn—2 sc.

Row 19: Ch 1, sc2tog, do not turn—1 sc.

Edging: Ch 1, sc 5 across row ends, sc 46 around unworked sts of Rnd 14, sc 5 across row ends, sc in sc of Row 19, join—57 sc.

Fasten off leaving a long tail for sewing. Sew Head Piece to top of Head with Row 19 resting between eyes. Weave in ends.

Horns (Make 2)

With **B** make a magic ring.

Rnd 1: 3 sc in ring—3 sc.

Rnds 2–16: Inc, sc around—18 sc at the end of Rnd 16.

Rnd 17: [Sc, inc, sc] around—24 sc.

Fasten off. Using a long length of **C**, embroider 4 lines, each a single loop, evenly around Horn using photos as a guide. Stuff Horn. Sew to top of Head on either side. Weave in ends.

Finishing

Sew inside edge of Sleeves together in front of the Body. Using **C** chain 60. Sew chain to sides of Dress Detail and looping behind where hands are joined. Weave in ends.

Mother Gothel

Designed by Valérie Prieur-Côté

Skill Level: Easy

When Mother Gothel is first seen in the tower with Rapunzel, there are several items that reveal Mother Gothel's true intentions, including a spinning wheel (as in *Sleeping Beauty* [1959]), a pattern of an apple (as in the Evil Queen's apple in *Snow White and the Seven Dwarfs* [1937]) on the bottom newel post of the stairway, and her lantern emitting a green color (reminiscent of Maleficent's magic, also in *Sleeping Beauty*).

Staying young and beautiful is such a chore. Luckily for Mother Gothel, she has discovered a special golden flower growing in a remote area of the kingdom that has magical powers to restore youth and health. Mother Gothel sets out to visit the secret location of the magical flower, only to discover that the King and Queen's guards have also discovered it . . . and they've taken it. They use the flower as medicine to save their ailing baby daughter, Rapunzel. This puts the flower's magic out of Mother Gothel's reach—briefly. Mother Gothel realizes the magic lives on in baby Rapunzel and decides there's only one thing left to do: take the child, hide her away, and raise Rapunzel herself. This way, Mother Gothel can keep the flower's magic close. No one must discover the truth, not even Rapunzel herself. This means Mother Gothel has a child to care for and parenting methods to learn! If her approach seems self-serving, narcissistic, and hyper-controlling, don't worry: As Gothel might say, "Mother knows best."

This pattern may be Mother Gothel's dream come true: a crochet version of herself that never ages! If she had her way, it may even be how she would prefer to be remembered. Her long black curls, her beautiful gown, her manipulative behavior . . . Maybe don't include that last detail, now that we think about it.

Mother Gothel [angrily]: "Enough with the lights, Rapunzel! You are not leaving this tower! Ever!" [sits down dramatically] "Great. Now I'm the bad guy."

—Mother Gothel to Rapunzel, *Tangled* (2010)

YARN

Worsted weight (#4 medium) yarn, shown in Lion Brand Basic Stitch Anti Pilling™ (100% acrylic, 185 yd. / 170 m per 3.5 oz. / 100 g skein)

Color A: #153 Black, 1 skein
Color B: #121L Almond, 1 skein
Color C: #138L Pomegranate, 1 skein
Color D: #158I Mustard, 1 skein

HOOK

US D (3.25 mm) crochet hook

NOTIONS

White embroidery thread
Pair of 9 mm black safety eyes
Stitch marker
Polyester stuffing
Yarn needle
Scissors

FINISHED MEASUREMENTS

Height: 9" / 22.5 cm
Width: 4" / 10 cm

SPECIAL STITCHES

Inc (increase) = Work 2 sc in next st.

Invdec (invisible single crochet decrease) = Insert hook in front loop only of each of next 2 sts, yo and draw through both sts, yo and draw through 2 loops on hook—1 st decreased.

Hdc-invdec (invisible half double crochet decrease) = Yo, insert hook in front loop only of each of next 2 sts, yo and draw through both sts, yo and draw through all loops on hook—1 st decreased.

Standing sc (standing sc) = With slipknot on hook, insert hook in indicated st, yo and draw up a loop, yo and draw through 2 loops on hook.

Bobble (bobble stitch) = [Yo, insert hook into st, yo and draw up a loop, yo and draw through 2 loops on hook] 4 times, yo and draw through all loops on hook.

Fsc (foundation single crochet) = With slipknot on hook, ch 2. Insert hook into 2nd ch from hook, yo and draw up a loop, yo and draw through 1 loop on hook *(foundation made)*, yo and draw through 2 loops on hook—1 Fsc completed. *Insert hook under the 2 loops of the foundation of previous Fsc, yo and draw up a loop, yo and draw through 1 loop on hook *(foundation made)*, yo and draw through 2 loops on hook—Fsc completed. Repeat from * until required number of Fsc are made.

Fhdc (foundation half double crochet) = With slipknot on hook, ch 2. Yo, insert hook into 2nd ch from hook, yo and draw up a loop, yo and draw through 1 loop on hook *(foundation made)*, yo and draw through 3 loops on hook—1 Fhdc completed. *Yo, insert hook under the 2 loops of the foundation of previous Fhdc, yo and draw up a loop, yo and draw through 1 loop on hook *(foundation made)*, yo and draw through 3 loops on hook—Fhdc completed. Repeat from * until required number of Fhdc are made.

GAUGE

28 sc and 28 rnds = 4 in. / 10 cm in sc

Gauge is not critical for this project. Ensure your stitches are tight so the stuffing won't show through.

NOTES

- Work in continuous rounds unless otherwise indicated.
- When indicated, join at the end of a round with a slip stitch in the first stitch. To join new yarn to a stitch, insert hook in stitch and pull up a loop in indicated color.
- To change colors, work the last yarn over of the previous stitch with the new color. Fasten off previous color unless otherwise indicated.
- If desired, instead of making a magic ring, chain 2 and work indicated stitches in the 2nd chain from the hook.

Arms (Make 2)

With **B**, make a magic ring.

Rnd 1: 4 sc in ring—4 sc.

Rnd 2: [Sc, inc] around—6 sc.

Rnd 3: [Sc 2, inc] around—8 sc.

Rnd 4: Sc around.

Rnd 5: Sc, bobble, sc 6.

Rnd 6: Sc around.

Rnd 7: [Sc 2, invdec] around—6 sc.

Rnds 8–18: Sc around.

Do not stuff.

Rnd 19: Ch 1, fold opening in half, working through both thicknesses, sc across—3 sc.

Fasten off.

Legs (Make 2)

With **A**, ch 6.

Rnd 1: Starting in 2nd ch from hook, sc 4, 4 sc in last ch, working in underside of chs, sc 3, 3 sc in last ch—14 sc.

Rnd 2: Sc 4, inc 4, sc 4, inc 2—20 sc.

Rnd 3: Working in BLO, sc around.

Rnd 4: Sc around.

Rnd 5: Sc 3, [invdec] 5 times, sc 7—15 sc.

Rnd 6: Sc, [invdec] 5 times, sc 4—10 sc.

Rnds 7–9: Sc around.

Change to **B**.

Rnds 10: Working in BLO, sc around.

Rnds 11–21: Sc around.

Change to **C**. (Change is optional to create underwear; continue with color **B** if desired.)

Rnd 22: Sc around, join.

Fasten off first Leg. Do not fasten off 2nd Leg. If necessary, work additional sc to shift start of round to middle of Leg's inner side. Continue to Body.

Body and Head

Hold Legs aligned, with toes facing same direction, to join in next rnd.

Rnd 1: Ch 1, sc around first Leg, sc in ch, sc around 2nd Leg, sc in underside of ch—22 sc.

Rnds 2–3: Sc around.

Change to **B**.

Rnds 4–7: Sc around.

Rnd 8: [Sc 3, invdec] 4 times, sc 2—18 sc.

Rnd 9: Sc around.

Rnd 10: [Sc 7, invdec] around—16 sc.

Rnd 11: [Sc 7, inc] around—18 sc.

Rnd 12: [Sc 4, inc, sc 3, inc] around—22 sc.

Rnds 13–14: Sc around.

Rnd 15: [Sc 4, invdec, sc 3, invdec] around—18 sc.

Rnd 16: [Sc 7, invdec] around—16 sc.

Hold Arms in position with Body to join in next rnd. Each Arm is joined by working through both the arm sts and body sts for 3 sts.

Rnd 17: Sc around Body, working through both Arm and Body sts at desired location to join.

Rnd 18: [Sc 2, invdec] around—12 sc.

Rnd 19: Sc around.

Rnd 20: [Invdec] 6 times—6 sc.

Rnd 21: Inc 6—12 sc.

Mother Gothel: "Rapunzel, look in that mirror. You know what I see? I see a strong, confident, beautiful young lady." [Rapunzel smiles]

Mother Gothel: "Oh, look, you're here, too."

—Mother Gothel to Rapunzel, *Tangled* (2010)

Rnd 22: [Sc, inc] around—18 sc.
Rnd 23: [Sc 2, inc] around—24 sc.
Rnd 24: Sc, inc, [sc 3, inc] 5 times, sc 2—30 sc.
Rnd 25: [Sc 4, inc] around—36 sc.
Rnds 26–33: Sc around.
Rnd 34: [Sc 4, invdec] around—30 sc.
Place eyes between Rnds 31 and 32, 5–6 stitches apart. You can also add the face details now or later.
Rnd 35: Sc, invdec, [sc 3, invdec] 5 times, sc 2—24 sc.
Rnd 36: [Sc 2, invdec] around—18 sc.
Rnd 37: [Sc, invdec] around—12 sc.
Stuff Head.
Rnd 38: Invdec around—6 sc.
Fasten off leaving a long tail for sewing. Sew remaining 6 sts closed. Weave in ends.

Face Details

With **B** embroider over 3 sts between eyes to form nose.
With **A** embroider eyebrows and eyelash using photo as a guide.
Using white embroidery floss add a little bit of white on the side of the eyes.

Dress

With **C**.
Rnd 1: FSC 20, making sure not to twist, join—20 sts.
Rnds 2–9: Sc around.
Rnd 10: Sc 5, inc, sc 8, inc, sc 5—22 sc.
Rnd 11: [Sc 6, inc] 3 times, sc—25 sc.
Rnd 12: [Sc 4, inc] around—30 sc.
Rnd 13: [Sc 5, inc] around—35 sc.

Rnd 14: [Sc 6, inc] around—40 sc.
Rnds 15–19: Sc around.
Rnd 20: [Sc 7, inc] around—45 sc.
Rnd 21: [Sc 8, inc] around—50 sc.
Rnd 22: [Sc 9, inc] around—55 sc.
Rnd 23: [Sc 10, inc] around—60 sc.
Rnd 24: [Sc 11, inc] around—65 sc.
Rnd 25: [Sc 12, inc] around—70 sc.
Rnd 26: [Sc 13, inc] around—75 sc.
Fasten off. Use beginning yarn tail to sew small gap at bottom of first rnd.

Sleeves (Make 2)

With **C**.
Row 1: On underside of Rnd 1 of Dress, join yarn, ch 7, skip 3 sts, sc, turn.
Rnd 2: Skip first sc, sc in each ch, sc in same st as join, rotating to work in skipped st on dress, sc in each skipped st on dress—11sc.
Rnds 3–6: Sc around.
If needed, work additional sc to shift start of rnd to middle of bottom of sleeve.
Rnd 7: Inc 2, sc 7, inc 2—15 sc.
Rnd 8: Inc 4, sc 7, inc 4—23 sc.
Change to **D**.
Rnd 9: Sc around.
Fasten off.
Work 2nd sleeve the same, with 6 unworked Dress sts between the 2 sleeves.

Collar

Join **D** at back of Dress. Sc around top of the dress, working into sc and underside of chs of Sleeves, join. Fasten off and weave in ends.

Belt Buckle

With **C**, make a magic ring.
Rnd 1: 8 sc in ring—8 sc.
Change to **D**.
Rnd 2: Sc around.
Fasten off, leaving a long tail for sewing.

Belt

With **C**.
Row 1: Fhdc 48—48 Fhdc.
Change to **D**.
Rnd 2: Sl st across, ch 1, working in underside of Fhdc, sl st across, ch 1, join.
Fasten off, leaving a long tail for sewing.
Using photo as a guide, wrap Belt around Dress. Using long tail, sew Belt on Dress. Sew Buckle in place on Belt.

Hair

With **A**.
[Ch 31, starting in 2nd ch from hook, sc across] 15 times—15 strands of hair, 30 sc on each strand.
Fasten off leaving a very long tail.
Using the tail, pass through one loop at end of each strand and pull to bring all the strands together. It will form a wig roughly in the shape of a U. If both sides of the U aren't touching, you can use the yarn to sew them together. Sew on Head.

Bangs

With **A**.
[Ch 6, starting in 2nd ch from hook sc across] twice—2 bangs, 5 sc on each bang.
Fasten of leaving a long tail. Sew on forehead of doll.

Finishing

Weave in remaining ends. If desired twist the ends of each strand of hair to make them curly.

Yzma

Designed by Lizette Coreano

Skill Level: Intermediate

There's a hidden clue to what's to come of Yzma's poisonous plans in *The Emperor's New Groove*. When she pours a poisoned drink onto a nearby cactus, if you keep watching, you'll see it takes the shape of a llama.

It's no wonder Yzma, former head administrator to the vain and cocky Emperor Kuzco, is planning to usurp the throne. The emperor did fire her after all. Now he plans to build an entire water park, dedicated to himself, to mark his birthday. It's not only excessive, it's downright negligent. Kuzco has to be stopped, and Yzma knows just the thing to get him out of the way. To keep her hands clean and avoid suspicion, she'll get her loyal assistant, Kronk, to remove Emperor Kuzco from the equation. Unfortunately, well-meaning Kronk can't quite be counted on, and instead of being poisoned, Kuzco is magically transformed into a llama. Not exactly the goal, but you know what? Yzma can work with this! If nothing else, she's a planner, and power is within her grasp . . .

Yzma may overthink her schemes a bit, but she never overthinks her outfit. A long black dress, gorgeous blue earrings, and purple feathers? She looks amazing! This crochet pattern is just the right size to put inside a box, put that box inside another box, mail it to yourself, and then open it to give it a cuddle. Or, you could keep it simple and just give it a cuddle?

"Ah, how shall I do it? Oh, I know. I'll turn him into a flea, a harmless, little flea, and then I'll put that flea in a box, and then I'll put that box inside of another box, and then I'll mail that box to myself, and when it arrives . . . I'll smash it with a hammer! It's brilliant, brilliant, brilliant, I tell you! Genius, I say! Or, to save on postage, I'll just poison him with this."

—Yzma, *The Emperor's New Groove* (2000)

YARN

Worsted weight (#4 medium) yarn, shown in:

Lion Brand Feels Like Butta (100% polyester, 218 yd. / 199m per 3.5 oz. / 100 g ball)

Color A: #215-147BA Quail, 1 ball

Color B: #215-153, Black, 1 ball

Lion Brand Color Theory (100% acrylic, 246 yd. / 225 m per 3.5 oz. / 100 g ball)

Color C: #147R Amethyst, 1 ball

Lion Brand Lazy Days™ (100% polyester, 179 yd. / 164 m per 3.5 oz. / 100 g ball)

Color D: #107N Bluebell, 1 ball

Lion Brand Vanna's Choice (100% acrylic, 170 yd. / 156 m per 3.5 oz. / 100 g ball)

Color E: #147B Purple, 1 ball

HOOK

US D (3.25 mm) crochet hook

1.65 mm steel crochet hook

NOTIONS

Pair of 12 mm black safety eyes

Black and silver embroidery thread

16-gauge wire

Wire cutters

Stitch markers

Polyester stuffing

Yarn needle

Scissors

FINISHED MEASUREMENTS

Height: 10.5" / 26.5 cm

Width: 4" / 10 cm

SPECIAL STITCHES

Inc (increase) = Work 2 sc in the next st.

Invdec (invisible single crochet decrease) = Insert hook in FLO of each of next 2 sts, yo and draw through both sts, yo and draw through 2 loops on hook—1 st decreased.

Popcorn (popcorn stitch) = Work 3 dc in next st, drop loop on hook, insert hook from front to back in first dc made, place dropped loop on hook and draw through dc.

Dc2tog (double crochet 2 together) = [Insert hook in next st, yo and draw up a loop, yo and draw through 2 loops on hook] twice, yo and draw through all loops on hook—1 st decreased.

Small Picot = Ch 2, sl st in last st made.

Large Picot = Ch 8, starting in the 2nd ch from the hook sl st 2, sc 2, hdc 2, dc.

Medium Picot = Ch 4, starting in the 2nd ch from hook, sl st 2, sk last ch.

GAUGE

24 sc and 27 rnds = 4 in. / 10 cm in sc

Gauge is not critical for this project. Ensure your stitches are tight so the stuffing won't show through.

NOTES

- Work in continuous rounds unless otherwise indicated.
- When indicated, join at the end of a round with a slip stitch in the first stitch.
- When changing colors, fasten off previous color unless otherwise indicated.
- For rounds worked in multiple colors, make the final yo of the stitch with the new color, and draw through with the new color to finish.
- Use larger hook unless otherwise indicated.

Fun Fact

There's a hidden clue to what's to come of Yzma's poisonous plans in *The Emperor's New Groove*. When she pours a poisoned drink onto a nearby cactus, if you keep watching, you'll see it takes the shape of a llama.

Arms (Make 2)

With **A** make a magic ring.

Rnd 1: 6 sc in ring—6 sts.

Rnd 2: Sc around.

Rnd 3: Sc 5, popcorn.

Rnds 4–16: Sc around.

Do not stuff. Fasten off. Set aside to join to Body.

Eyelashes (Make 2)

With black embroidery floss and 1.65 mm hook, make a magic ring.

Rnd 1: 10 sc in ring, turn—10 sc.

Do not close ring too tight, you will need to get the safety eye through the center.

Rnd 2: [Ch 7, starting in the 2nd ch from the hook, sl st 6, sl st into the next 2 sc on Rnd 1] 4 times—4 Eyelashes.

Fasten off, place onto the safety eyes, using photo as a guide. Tighten the ring, weave in the ends. Set aside for later.

Legs (Make 2)

With **B** make a magic ring.

Rnd 1: 6 sc in ring—6 sts.

Rnd 2: Inc 2, (hdc, dc) in next st, (dc, hdc) in next st, inc 2—12 sts.

Rnd 3: Working in BLO, sc around.

Change to **A**. Fasten off **B** leaving a long tail hanging out for shoe strap.

Rnd 4: Working in BLO, sc 4, [dc2tog] twice, sc 4—10 sts.

Rnd 5: Sc around.

Rnd 6: Invdec, sc 8—9 sts.

Rnd 7: Invdec, sc 7—8 sts.

Rnds 8–17: Sc around.

Fasten off first Leg. Do not fasten off 2nd Leg.

Using st markers, mark first st of 2nd Leg and corresponding st of inner Leg on first Leg (dc2tog sts are at the front of foot).

Rnd 18: Ch 2, sc in marked st on first Leg, sc in remaining sts around first Leg, sc in each ch, sc around 2nd Leg, sc in underside of 2 chs—20 sts.

Rnd 19: Sc 9, inc 2, sc 9—22 sc.

Rnd 20: Sc around.

Rnd 21: [Sc 9, invdec] twice—20 sc.

Change to **B**.

Rnd 22: Sc around.

With the tail of **B** left after Rnd 3 of Legs, sew a line for the shoe strap.

Rnd 23: [Invdec] 10 times—10 sts.

Rnd 24: Working in BLO, sc around.

Rnds 25–27: Sc around.

Rnd 28: 2 hdc in next st, sc, 2 hdc in next st, sc 7—12 sts.

Rnd 29: Invdec, sc, invdec, sc 7—10 sts.

Begin working with multiple colors on the next rnd. Do not fasten off when changing colors until indicated.

Rnd 30: With **B** sc, with **A** sc, with **B** sc 8.

Hold Arms in line with Body to join on next rnd.

Rnd 31: With **A** sc 5 on Body, sc in closest st on first Arm, sc 5 around Arm, continuing on Body, with **B** sc

4, **A** sc, sc in closest st on 2nd Arm, sc 5 around Arm—22 sc.

Fasten off **B**. Continue with **A**.

Cut 2 lengths of wire to reach from foot to neck. Bend the ends of the wire. Insert into feet.

Cut 2 lengths of wire for arms. Bend the ends of the wire. Insert into the arms. Stuff Legs and Body, using stick as necessary to stuff the Legs.

Continue with **BODY**.

Rnd 32: [Sc 3, invdec] 4 times, sc 2—18 sc.

Rnd 33: [Invdec] 9 times—9 sc.

Rnds 34–35: Sc around.

Rnd 36: Working in BLO, sc around.

DO NOT fasten off.

With **B**, embroider 2 lines for the dress straps, starting from Rnd 30 and over the shoulders and into the top **B** edge of the dress.

Collar

With doll upside down, working in unworked FL on Rnd 35 of Body, skip center 3 FL, join **C** in next FL. Crochet over the tail end as you go.

Row 1: Ch 2 (*does not count as a st here and throughout*), working in unworked FLO, 2 dc in next 6 sts, turn—12 sts.

Row 2: Ch 2, 2 dc in each st, turn—24 sts.

Row 3: Medium picot, working in FLO, sc, [large picot, sk 1 st, (sl st, medium picot, hdc) in next st, sc] 3 times, sc, [large picot, sk 1 st, (sl st, medium picot, hdc) in next st,

sc] 3 times, large picot, sk 1 st, sl st, medium picot, hdc, sl st, turn—15 picots.
Row 4: Working in unused BL of Row 2, sl st 1, [large picot, sk 1 st, (sl st, medium picot, hdc) in next st, sc] 7 times, large picot, sk 1, sl st.
Fasten off, weave in the end.
Steam block to uncurl the collar by pinning the longer spikes from Rows 3 and 4 together.

Second Collar

With **B**.
Row 1: Ch 9, starting in the 2nd ch from hook, sc across, turn—8 sts.
Row 2: Ch 2, dc, sc, sl st, sc, picot, sl st 2, sc, dc.
Fasten off with a long tail.
Wrap around neck with picot point facing down. Sew the ends together. Weave in ends.

Skirt

With **B** and doll upside down, join yarn in last unworked FL on Rnd 23 of Body.
Rnd 1: Ch 1, working in unworked FLO, inc around—20 sts.
Rnd 2: [Sc, inc] 10 times—30 sts.
Rnd 3: Sc around.
Rnd 4: [Sc 4, invdec] 5 times—25 sts.
Rnds 5–8: Sc around. At end of Rnd 8, join.
Fasten off.
Begin working in rows. Skip first 2 sts, join yarn in next st.
Row 9: Ch 1, sc 24, turn leaving last st unworked—24 sts.
Row 10: Ch 1, invdec, sc 20, invdec, turn—22 sts.
Row 11: Ch 1, sc 20, invdec, turn—21 sts.
Row 12: Ch 1, invdec, sc 19, turn—20 sts.
Row 13: Ch 1, sc 18, invdec, turn—19 sts.
Row 14: Ch 1, invdec, sc 17, turn—18 sts.
Rows 15–23: Ch 1, sc across, turn.
Row 24: Ch 1, invdec, sc 14, invdec, turn—16 sts.
Row 25: Ch 1, sc 6, [inc, sc] twice, inc, sc 5, turn—19 sts.
Row 26: Ch 1, inc 2, [sc 2, inc] 5 times, sc 2, turn—26 sts.
Row 27: Ch 1, sc, [inc, sc 3] 6 times, sc, turn—32 sts.
Row 28: Ch 1, sc 8, inc, sc 3, inc, sc 2, inc 2, sc 2, inc, sc 3, inc, sc 8, turn—38 sts.
Rows 29–30: Ch 1, sc across, turn.
Fasten off. Weave in ends.

Resume Head

Continue with **A**.
Rnd 37: [Inc, sc 2] 3 times—12 sts.
Rnd 38: Inc around—24 sts.
Rnd 39: [Sc 2, inc] 8 times—32 sts.
Rnd 40: [Sc 4, inc] 6 times, sc 2—38 sts.
Rnds 41–45: Sc around.
Rnd 46: [Sc 10, invdec] 3 times, sc 2—35 sts.
Rnds 47–53: Sc around.
Insert safety eyes between Rnds 43 and 44, 8 sts between the eyes, centered with the head.
Cut wire for Head: Curl the end of the wire. About 1.25" up, bend the wire into an L shape. Cut the wire about 8" from the bend and bend it into a coil shape. Put the beginning end all the way down into the Body.
Rnd 54: [Sc 9, invdec] 3 times, sc 2—32 sts.
Rnd 55: [Sc 2, invdec] 8 times—24 sts.
Stuff Head firmly.
Rnd 56: Sc 2, [invdec] 5 times, sc 2, [invdec] 5 times—14 sts.
Rnd 57: [Invdec] 7 times—7 sts.
Fasten off and close the hole by sewing through FLO of all 7 sc.

Ears

Facing the front of the doll, start with the Left Ear first. Starting 5 sts back from the eye, insert hook between Rnds 45 and 46 into doll and then back out 2 rows down. Grab **A** and pull it all the way through (1 loop on hook). Yo and draw through loop on hook to form a ring. Make 5 hdc into the ring, making sure *to hold the beginning tail end down to keep it tight.* Fasten off, tighten the loop, tie the ends together, weave in the ends.
Repeat for the Right Ear, inserting hook into doll between Rnds 43 and 44 and out 2 rows up.

Headpiece

With **E** make a magic ring.

Rnd 1: 4 sc in ring—4 sts.

Rnd 2: Sc around.

Rnd 3: [Inc, sc] twice—6 sts.

Rnd 4: [Inc, sc] 3 times—9 sts.

Rnds 5–6: Sc around.

Rnd 7: [Inc, sc] 4 times, inc—14 sts.

Rnd 8: [Inc, sc 6] twice—16 sts.

Rnd 9: [Sc 7, inc] twice—18 sts.

Rnd 10: [Inc, sc 8] twice—20 sts.

Rnds 11–16: Sc around.

Rnd 17: [Invdec, sc 8] twice—18 sts.

Rnd 18: [Sc 7, invdec] twice—16 sts.

Rnds 19–48: Sc around. At end of Rnd 48, join.

Change to **B**.

Rnd 49: Working in BLO, sc around.

Rnds 50–53: Sc around.

Cut a piece of wire a little longer than the **E** feather. Curl the end so the wire doesn't poke through.

Slide it all the way into the tip of the feather with the curled end first.

Flatten the **E** section of the feather.

Stuff the last 1.25" of the feather to make it round.

Rnd 54: [Inc, sc] 8 times—24 sc.

Rnd 55: [Inc, sc 2] 8 times—32 sc.

Rnd 56: [Sc 3, inc] 8 times—40 sc.

Rnds 57–62: Sc around.

Rnd 63: Sc 7, dc, tr, dtr, picot, tr, dc, sc 28.

Begin working in rows.

Rnd 64: Sl st in the next st, turn, sc 20, sl st—20 sc.

Fasten off leaving a long tail to sew to Head.

Sew to Head with point centered between eyes, covering Rnd 47 of the Head. The sides should be touching the Ears.
With **E**, embroider a line behind the eyelashes for the eyeshadow.

Earrings (Make 2)

With **D** make a magic ring.
Rnd 1: 6 hdc in ring—6 sts.
Rnd 2: [Inc, sc] 3 times, join—9 sts.
Insert hook from the back of the Ear into the st where the piercing would be on the earlobe.
Sl st the Earring to the Ear.
Fasten off, weave in ends.
Repeat on other Ear.

Dagger

With 1.65 mm hook.
Strap: With black floss, ch 15 or enough to wrap around thigh, wrap around her thigh, sl st to the first ch, fasten off. It shouldn't be too tight so you can slip the knife in it.
With black floss, make a magic ring.
Rnd 1: 6 sc in ring—6 sts.
Rnd 2: Working in BLO, sc around.
Rnds 3–4: Sc around.
Rnd 5: Working in FLO, [inc, sc] 3 times—9 sts.
Rnd 6: [Inc, sc] 4 times, sc—13 sts.
Change to silver floss.
Rnd 7: Working in BLO, sc around.
Rnd 8: [Invdec, sc 4] twice, sc—11 sts.
Rnd 9: [Sc 3, invdec] twice, sc—9 sts.
Rnd 10: Sc around.
Rnd 11: [Invdec, sc 2] twice, sc—7 sts.

Rnds 12–13: Sc around.
Rnd 14: [Sc, invdec] twice, sc—5 sts.
Fasten off. Sew closed remaining sts. Weave in the end.
Flatten the Dagger, slip into the Leg strap.

"What? A llama? He's supposed to be dead!"
—Yzma, *The Emperor's New Groove* (2000)

Madam Mim

Designed by Lee Sartori

Skill Level: Beginner

Madam Mim is powerful. Arguably the most powerful witch in the land. Everyone knows it, but for some frustrating reason, Mim's rival, the wizard Merlin, seems to think that Mim is a sham. It's honestly pretty rude. Now Merlin has taken on a student, some boy named Wart, and is teaching him magic. Who does he think he is? After *gently* trying to persuade Merlin to stop his pursuits by way of some light mischief, their conflict comes down to a duel. Here Mim intends to best Merlin once and for all. She'll show off her talent for shape-shifting, transforming into a cat, a crocodile, a fox, a chicken, an elephant, a tiger, a snake, and even a rhinoceros (all with purple hair, of course). She'll end her impressive performance by transforming into a menacing, purple dragon. Can Merlin do that? Madam Mim will win, and Merlin will have to slink into anonymity. At least, that's the plan.

Mim is a small witch with shoulder-length lavender hair and green eyes. She wears an indigo shirt, a magenta skirt, dark magenta sleeves, and violet shoes. As a witch who can shape-shift, she can take on any shape she desires, but we appreciate her commitment to a fun and vibrant color scheme! This crochet version likely won't change into a purple dragon, but we offer no guarantees.

"Sounds like someone's sick. How lovely, heh. I do hope it's serious. Something dreadful."

—Madam Mim, *The Sword in the Stone* (1963)

YARN

Worsted weight (#4 medium) yarn, shown in WeCrochet Swish (100% fine superwash merino wool, 110 yd. / 100 m per 1.75 oz. / 50 g ball)

Color A: Amethyst Heather, 1 ball

Color B: Karma Heather, 1 ball

Color C: Allium, 1 ball

Color D: Crush, 1 ball

Color E: Nutmeg Heather, 1 ball

HOOK

US D (3.25 mm) crochet hook

NOTIONS

Pair of 6 mm black safety eyes

White felt

Lime green felt

Plastic mesh

2 bamboo rods, 4 mm diameter

Black embroidery thread

Stitch markers

Polyester stuffing

Yarn needle

Scissors

FINISHED MEASUREMENTS

Height: 10" / 25 cm

Width: 8" / 20 cm

SPECIAL STITCHES

Inc (increase) = Work 2 sc in the next st.

Invdec (invisible single crochet decrease) = Insert hook in front loop only of each of next 2 sts, yo and draw through both sts, yo and draw through 2 loops on hook—1 st decreased.

Sc2tog (single crochet 2 together) = [Insert hook in next st, yo and draw up a loop] twice, yo and draw through all loops on hook—1 st decreased.

Popcorn (popcorn stitch) = Work 5 dc in next st, drop loop on hook, insert hook from front to back in first dc made, place dropped loop on hook and draw through dc.

GAUGE

28 sc and 28 rnds = 4 in. / 10 cm in sc

Gauge is not critical for this project. Ensure your stitches are tight so the stuffing won't show through.

NOTES

- Work in continuous rounds unless otherwise indicated.
- When indicated, join at the end of a round with a slip stitch in the first stitch. To join new yarn to a stitch, insert hook in stitch and pull up a loop in indicated color.
- To change colors, work the last yarn over of the previous stitch with the new color. Fasten off previous color unless otherwise indicated.
- If desired, instead of making a magic ring, chain 2 and work indicated stitches in the 2nd chain from the hook.

Fun Fact

In *The Sword in the Stone* (1963), the roof of Madam Mim's house was designed to resemble a witch's black hat.

Boot Soles (Make 4)

With **A**.

Rnd 1: Ch 7, starting in 2nd ch from hook, sc 5, 3 sc in last ch, rotate to work in underside of ch, sc 5, 3 sc in skipped ch—16 sc.

Rnd 2: *Sc 5, [inc] 3 times; repeat from * around—22 sc.

Fasten off first Sole, do not fasten off 2nd Sole. Place first Sole on plastic mesh, trace and cut shape of Sole. Cut out plastic and insert between 2 Soles.

Rnd 3: Working through both thicknesses, sc around Sole—22 sc.

Continue to Boot.

Boots (Make 2)

With **A**.

Rnd 1: Sc 5, [invdec] 3 times, sc 11—19 sc.

Rnd 2: Sc 5, [invdec] 3 times, sc 8—16 sc.

Rnd 3: Sc 3, [invdec] 3 times, sc 7—13 sc.

Rnd 4: Sc 2, [invdec] 3 times, sc 5—10 sc.

Rnd 5: Sc around.

Fasten off. Stuff Boot lightly.

Legs (Make 2)

With **B** join to st at back of Boot in BL.

Rnd 1: [Sc2tog, sc] twice, [sc2tog] twice—6 sc.

Rnds 2–8: Sc around.

With **C** join to back of Leg in FL.

Rnd 9: Working in FLO, ch 6, sl st in first st, [sl st, (sl st, ch 6, sl st) in next st] twice, sl st—3 ch-6 Ruffles.

Rnd 10: Ch 1, working in unworked BL of Rnd 8 sts, inc around—12 sc.

Rnd 11: [Inc, sc] around—18 sc.

Rnd 12: [Sc, inc, sc] around—24 sc.

Rnd 13: [Inc, sc 3] around—30 sc.

Fasten off first Leg. Do not fasten off 2nd Leg. Using 2 st markers mark center sc at inner thigh of each Leg.

Rnd 14: Sc around to first marked st, sc in marked st, sc in marked st on first Leg to join, sc around first Leg, sc in remaining sc of 2nd Leg—60 sc.

Rnds 15–29: Sc around.

Fasten off **C**.

Insert Bamboo Rod into each Leg for support. Stuff Tops of Legs and Body. Continue stuffing as work progresses.

With **A** join to st at back of Body in BL.

Rnd 30: Ch 1, working in BLO, sc around, join—60 sc.

Rnd 31: Ch 1 tightly, sc around, do not join.

Rnds 32–34: Sc around.
Rnd 35: [Sc 4, invdec, sc 4] around—54 sc.
Rnd 36: [Invdec, sc 7] around—48 sc.
Rnd 37: [Sc 3, invdec, sc 3] around—42 sc.
Rnd 38: [Invdec, sc 5] around—36 sc.
Rnd 39: [Sc 2, invdec, sc 2] around—30 sc.
Rnd 40: [Invdec, sc 3] around—24 sc.
Fasten off. Continue to Head.

Head

With **E** join to back of Body in BL.
Rnd 1: Ch 1, working in BLO sc around, join—24 sc.
Rnd 2: Ch 1, sc around, join.
Rnd 3: Ch 1 tightly, inc around, do not join—48 sc.
Rnd 4: [Inc, sc 7] around—54 sc.
Rnds 5–18: Sc around.
Using felt add a circle of lime green around safety eye. Add a layer of white felt behind green using photos as a guide. Add eyes between Rows 15 and 16 of Head approximately 5 sts apart. Embroider nose between Rnds 14 and 15 over 4 sts. Stuff Head and continue stuffing as work progresses.
Rnd 19: [Invdec, sc 7] around—48 sc.
Rnd 20: [Sc 3, invdec, sc 3] around—42 sc.
Rnd 21: [Invdec, sc 5] around—36 sc.
Rnd 22: [Sc 2, invdec, sc 2] around—30 sc.
Rnd 23: [Invdec, sc 3] around—24 sc.
Rnd 24: [Sc, invdec, sc] around—18 sc.
Rnd 25: [Invdec, sc] around—12 sc.
Rnd 26: Invdec around—6 sc.
Fasten off, leaving a long tail for sewing. Sew remaining 6 sts closed. Weave in ends.

Skirt

With doll upside down, with **D**, join in unworked FL at back of Body on Rnd 29.
Rnd 1: Ch 1, working in unworked FLO, sc around, join—60 sc.
Rnd 2: [Inc, sc 9] around—66 sc.
Rnds 3–4: Sc around.
Rnd 5: [Sc 5, inc, sc 5] around—72 sc.
Rnds 6–7: Sc around.
Rnd 8: [Inc, sc 11] around—78 sc.
Rnds 9–10: Sc around.
Rnd 11: [Sc 6, inc, sc 6] around—84 sc.
Rnds 12–13: Sc around.
Rnd 14: [Inc, sc 13] around—90 sc.
Rnds 15–17: Sc around.
Rnd 18: Working in BLO, sl st in each st around, join.
Fasten off. Weave in ends.

Arms (Make 2)

With **E** make a magic ring.
Rnd 1: 6 sc in ring—6 sc.
Rnd 2: Inc around—12 sc.
Rnds 3–4: Sc around.
Rnd 5: Popcorn, sc 11.
Rnds 6–7: Sc around.
Rnd 8: Invdec around—6 sc.
Rnds 9–16: Sc around.
Join with **B** in FL of any st.
Rnd 17: Working in FLO ch 1, inc around, join—12 sc.
Rnds 18–19: Ch 1, working in BLO sc around, join.
Rnd 20: Ch 1 tightly, sc around, do not join.
Rnds 21–28: Inc, sc around—20 sc at end of Rnd 28.
Sl st in next st, stuff top of Arm. Pinch in half and sc across through both thicknesses to close. Fasten off leaving a long tail for sewing. Sew Arm to Top of Body. Weave in ends.

Hair Crown

With **C** make a magic ring. Work in BLO for entire piece.
Rnd 1: 6 sc in ring—6 sc.
Rnd 2: Inc around—12 sc.
Rnd 3: [Inc, sc] around—18 sc.
Rnd 4: [Sc, inc, sc] around—24 sc.
Rnd 5: [Inc, sc 3] around—30 sc.
Rnd 6: [Sc 2, inc, sc 2] around—36 sc.
Rnd 7: [Inc, sc 5] around—42 sc.
Rnd 8: [Sc 3, inc, sc 3] around—48 sc.
Rnd 9: [Inc, sc 7] around—54 sc.
Fasten off leaving a long tail for sewing. Sew Hair Crown to top of Head.

Finishing

Using **C**, cut approximately 90 pieces of hair measuring 10" long. Working in every 3rd st around Hair Crown, attach strand to unworked FL with lark's head knot. Using photos as a guide trim hair around head.
Using a length of **C**, tie a bow around the bottom of the bloomers on each Leg, right above the Ruffles.

Chernabog

Designed by Lee Sartori

Skill Level: Easy

Chernabog—an enormous, winged demon with menacing eyes and fearsome horns—is ready for some amusement. He waits with anticipation atop Bald Mountain for the creatures below to sing and dance for him . . . until they drop. As the night goes on, no one stops, for fear of displeasing the tyrannical giant watching from above. The party could go on forever, it seems. That is, until the pesky ringing of the church bells in the village and the beautiful streaks of daylight breaking on the horizon signal the coming dawn. It's all too much for Chernabog to bear. Disgusted, he folds his wings back over his body to protect himself from the sunlight. Then, he hides himself away in Bald Mountain, with his horde of lost souls, to await the next Walpurgis Night . . .

Chernabog may not be pleased with this amigurumi version of him. We gave him his fearsome horns and his giant wings, but he just looks so . . . cute! Consider playing some soothing music while crocheting this one, to see if it changes his attitude. If you're racing to finish this one, remember that tomorrow's another day . . . and that means another night!

"Under his spell, they dance furiously until the coming of dawn and the sounds of church bells send the infernal army slinking back into their abodes of darkness."

—Composer and Film's Narrator Deems Taylor,
describing Chernabog's scenes in *Fantasia* (1940)

YARN

Worsted weight (#4 medium) yarn, shown in Lion Brand Basic Stitch Anti Pilling™ (100% acrylic, 185 yd. / 170 m per 3.5 oz. / 100 g skein)

Color A: #153 Black, 3 skeins

Color B: #112S Deco Rose, 1 skein

HOOK

US D (3.25 mm) crochet hook

NOTIONS

Yellow felt
Glue
Stitch markers
Polyester stuffing
Yarn needle
Scissors

FINISHED MEASUREMENTS

Height: 14" / 35 cm
Width: 14" / 35 cm

SPECIAL STITCHES

Fpsc (front post single crochet) = Insert hook from front to back to front again around post of next st, yo and draw up a loop, yo and draw through 2 loops.

Bpsc (back post single crochet) = Insert hook from back to front to back again around post of next st, yo and draw up a loop, yo and draw through 2 loops.

Inc (increase) = Work 2 sc in the next st.

Invdec (invisible single crochet decrease) = Insert hook in front loop only of each of next 2 sts, yo and draw through both sts, yo and draw through 2 loops on hook—1 st decreased.

Popcorn (popcorn stitch) = Work 5 dc in next st, drop loop on hook, insert hook from front to back in first dc made, place dropped loop on hook and draw through dc.

GAUGE

28 sc and 28 rnds = 4 in. / 10 cm in sc

Gauge is not critical for this project. Ensure your stitches are tight so the stuffing won't show through.

NOTES

- Work in continuous rounds unless otherwise indicated.
- When indicated, join at the end of a round with a slip stitch in the first stitch. To join new yarn to a stitch, insert hook in stitch and pull up a loop in indicated color.
- To change colors, work the last yarn over of the previous stitch with the new color. Fasten off previous color unless otherwise indicated.
- If desired, instead of making a magic ring, chain 2 and work indicated stitches in the 2nd chain from the hook.

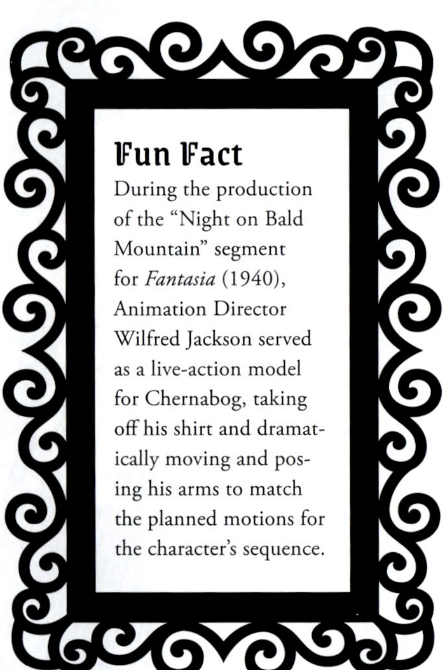

Fun Fact

During the production of the "Night on Bald Mountain" segment for *Fantasia* (1940), Animation Director Wilfred Jackson served as a live-action model for Chernabog, taking off his shirt and dramatically moving and posing his arms to match the planned motions for the character's sequence.

Arms (Make 2)

With **A**, make a magic ring.
Rnd 1: 6 sc in ring—6 sc.
Rnd 2: Inc around—12 sc.
Rnds 3–4: Sc around.
Rnd 5: Popcorn, sc 11.
Rnds 6–9: Sc around.
Rnd 10: Inc, sc around—13 sc.
Rnd 11: Sc around.
Rnd 12: Inc, sc around—14 sc.
Rnd 13: Sc around.
Rnd 14: Inc, sc around—15 sc.
Rnds 15–20: Sc around.
Fasten off. Stuff. Set aside to join to Body.

Mountain Base

With **A**, make a magic ring.
Rnd 1: 8 sc in ring—8 sc.
Rnd 2: Inc around—16 sc.
Rnd 3: [Inc, sc] around—24 sc.
Rnd 4: [Sc, inc, sc] around—32 sc.
Rnd 5: [Inc, sc 3] around—40 sc.
Rnd 6: [Sc 2, inc, sc 2] around—48 sc.
Rnd 7: [Inc, sc 5] around—56 sc.
Rnd 8: [Sc 3, inc, sc 3] around—64 sc.
Rnd 9: [Inc, sc 7] around—72 sc.
Rnd 10: [Sc 4, inc, sc 4] around, join—80 sc.
Rnd 11: Ch 1, working in BLO sc around, join.
Rnds 12–16: Ch 1, sc around, join.
Rnd 17: [Ch 4, skip next 8 sc, sc 32] twice, join—64 sc, 2 ch-4 sps.
Rnd 18: Ch 1, [sc in next 4 chs, sc 32] twice, join—72 sc.
Rnds 19–20: Ch 1, sc around, join.

Rnd 21: Ch 1, sc 14, ch 8, skip 16 sts, sc 42, join—56 sc, 1 ch-8 sps.
Rnd 22: Ch 1, sc 14, sc in next 8 chs, sc 42, join—64 sc.
Rnds 23–25: Ch 1, sc around, join.
Rnd 26: Ch 1, sc 42, ch 8, skip 16 sts, sc 6, join—48 sc, 1 ch-8 sps.
Rnd 27: Ch 1, sc 42, sc in next 8 chs, sc 6, join—56 sc.
Rnd 28: Ch 1, [ch 4, skip 8 sts, sc 20] twice, join—40 sc, 2 ch-4 spaces.
Rnd 29: Ch 1, [sc in next 4 chs, sc 20] twice, join—48 sc.
Rnds 30–32: Ch 1, sc around, join.
Rnd 33: Ch 1, bpsc around, join.
Rnd 34: Ch 1, [sc 3, invdec, sc 3] around, join—42 sc.
Rnd 35: Ch 1, [invdec, sc 5] around, join—36 sc.
Stuff. Continue to Body.

Body

Continuing with **A**.

Rnd 1: Ch 1 tightly, sc around, do not join—36 sc.
Rnd 2: [Inc, sc 11] 3 times—39 sc.
Rnd 3: [Sc 6, inc, sc 6] 3 times—42 sc.
Rnd 4: [Inc, sc 13] 3 times—45 sc.
Rnd 5: [Sc 7, inc, sc 7] 3 times—48 sc.
Rnd 6: [Inc, sc 15] 3 times—51 sc.
Rnd 7: [Sc 8, inc, sc 8] 3 times—54 sc.
Hold Arms in line with Body to join in next rnd.
Rnd 8: Sc 15 around Arm to join, sc 27 on Body, sc 15 around 2nd Arm to join, sc 27 on Body—84 sc.
Rnds 9–11: Sc around.
Rnd 12: [Sc 6, invdec, sc 6] around—78 sc.
Rnd 13: [Invdec, sc 11] around—72 sc.
Rnd 14: [Sc 5, invdec, sc 5] around—66 sc.
Rnd 15: [Invdec, sc 9] around—60 sc.
Rnd 16: [Sc 4, invdec, sc 4] around—54 sc.
Rnd 17: [Invdec, sc 7] around—48 sc.
Rnd 18: [Sc 3, invdec, sc 3] around—42 sc.
Rnd 19: [Invdec, sc 5] around—36 sc.
Rnd 20: [Sc 2, invdec, sc 2] around—30 sc.
Stuff Body firmly paying attention to stuffing shoulders. Continue to Head.

Head

Continuing with **A**.

Rnd 1: Sc around—30 sc.
Rnd 2: Ch 1 tightly, [sc 4, invdec, sc 4] around, do not join—27 sc.
Rnd 3: [Invdec, sc 7] around—24 sc.
Rnd 4: Sc around.
Rnd 5: [Inc, sc] around—36 sc.
Rnd 6: Fpsc around.
Rnds 7–19: Sc around.
Stuff Head, continue stuffing as work progresses.
Rnd 20: [Sc 2, invdec, sc 2] around—30 sc.
Rnd 21: [Invdec, sc 3] around—24 sc.
Rnd 22: [Sc, invdec, sc] around—18 sc.
Rnd 23: [Invdec, sc] around—12 sc.
Rnd 24: Invdec around—6 sc.
Fasten off leaving a long tail for sewing. Sew remaining 6 sts closed. Weave in ends.

Ears (Make 2)

With **A**, make a magic ring.

Rnd 1: 6 sc in ring—6 sc.
Rnd 2: Inc 4, 2 hdc in next st, 2 dc in last st—12 sts.
Fasten off leaving a long tail for sewing. Sew to sides of Head.

Horns (Make 2)

With **A**, make a magic ring.

Rnd 1: 3 sc in ring—3 sc.
Rnds 2–13: Inc, sc around—15 sc at end of Rnd 13.
Rnd 14: [Sc 2, inc, sc 2] around—18 sc.
Fasten off leaving a long tail for sewing. Stuff Horn. Sew to sides of Head above Ears. Weave in ends.

Small Mountain Spikes (Make 4)

With **A**, make a magic ring.

Rnd 1: 6 sc in ring, join—6 sc.
Rnd 2: Ch 1 tightly, working in BLO inc, sc 5, do not join—7 sc.
Rnds 3–7: Inc, sc around—12 sc at end of Rnd 7.
Fasten off leaving a long tail for sewing. Do not stuff. Sew to ch-4 sps of Mountain Base using the underside of the ch-4, and the 8 skipped sts of the round below. Weave in ends.

Large Mountain Spike (Make 2)

With **A**, make a magic ring.

Rnd 1: 3 sc in ring—3 sc.

Rnds 2–10: Inc, sc around—12 sc at end of Rnd 10.

Rnd 11: [Inc, sc 3] around—15 sc.

Rnd 12: [Sc 2, inc, sc 2] around—18 sc.

Rnd 13: [Inc, sc 5] around—21 sc.

Rnd 14: [Sc 3, inc, sc 3] around—24 sc.

Rnds 15–18: Sc around.

Fasten off leaving a long tail for sewing. Stuff Spike. Sew to ch-8 sps of Mountain Base using the underside of the ch-8 and the 16 skipped sts of the round below. Weave in ends.

Wings (Make 2 with A and 2 with B)

Row 1 (WS): Ch 21, starting in 2nd ch from hook sc across, turn—20 sc.

Work in BLO for remaining rows.

Row 2: Ch 1, inc 2, sc across to last 2 sts, inc 2, turn—24 sc.

Row 3: Ch 1, sc across, turn.

Rows 4–25: Repeat Rows 2–3—68 sc at end of Row 25.

Row 26: Repeat Row 2—72 sc.

Rows 27–32: Ch 1, sc 12, hdc 12, dc 24, hdc 12, sc 12, turn.

Fasten off **B**. Do not fasten off **A**. Place a **B** wing on top of an **A** wing. Next round will join wings together.

Rnd 33 (joining): With **A**, ch 1, sc through both thicknesses of each row end and st around, join.

Fasten off. Weave in ends.

Wing Ribbing

With **A**, sl st to top edge of wing, ch 1, sc in unworked FL of sts left between Rows 5 and 6, 11 and 12, 17 and 18, 23 and 24, and 29 and 30, leaving a ch-4 tail at the end of each rib before fastening off.

Sew Wings to back of Body. Weave in ends.

Eyebrow

With **A**, ch 20.

Fasten off leaving a long tail for sewing.

Finishing

Using yellow felt, cut eyes and glue to front of Head. Using tail of Eyebrow, sew Eyebrow above eyes using photos as a guide. Weave in ends.

Abbreviations

BL or **BLO**=back loop or back loop only

ch(s)=chain stitch(es)

dc=double crochet

dc2tog=double crochet 2 stitches together

dec=decrease

exsc=extended single crochet

FL or **FLO**=front loop or front loop only

hdc=half double crochet

hdc2tog=half double crochet 2 stitches together

inc=increase

rep=repeat

rnd=round

RS=right side

sc=single crochet

sc2tog=single crochet 2 stitches together

sk=skip

sl st=slip stitch

sp=space

st(s)=stitch(es)

tr=treble crochet

WS=wrong side

yo=yarn over

Yarn Resources

Lion Brand Yarn: www.lionbrand.com

WeCrochet Yarn: www.crochet.com

Yarn Citizen: www.yarncitizen.com

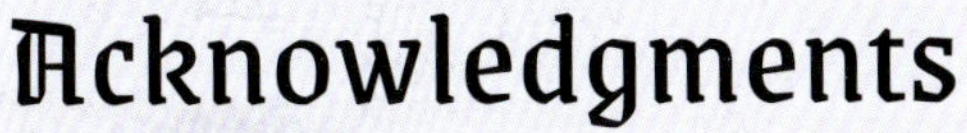

Acknowledgments

Disney Villains Amigurumi has been one of my favorite projects that I have worked on, and it helped that I had some of my wonderful friends share in the excitement. I would like to thank fellow designers Anna Leyzina, Sarah Csiacsek, Elise Speed, Zac Doar, Valérie Prieur-Côté, Lizette Coreano, and Nicole Rogowski for their amazing work. I would also love to thank my friends at Lion Brand Yarn, WeCrochet, and Furls Crochet for their support for this title. Thanks also to the Walt Disney Animation Research Library and the Walt Disney Archives. Thank you to my husband, Sean, and my sons, Noël and Conan, for listening to all of my written entries about the villains, and all the fun facts I discovered about each one. And last but not least, thank you to my editor Alexis Sattler for making this project an amazing experience.

Author Biography

Lee Sartori is the crochet designer behind CoCo Crochet Lee. Author of several popular crochet books, she can be seen as a guest host on the popular PBS/Create TV show *Knit and Crochet Now!*, and a featured instructor on Skillshare, where she demonstrates fun crochet skills and patterns. Lee's passion is designing modern, wearable garments and adorable amigurumi. Lee lives in Halifax, Canada, with her two children, Noël and Conan; her amazing husband, Sean; her adorable bunny, Neville, and her two cats, Ginny and Toast. You can find her work on her blog and on social media, where she posts fun and whimsical takes on crochet.

PO Box 3088
San Rafael, CA 94912
www.insighteditions.com

Find us on Facebook: www.facebook.com/InsightEditions
Follow us on Instagram: @insighteditions

ISBN: 979-8-3374-0098-3

Publisher: Raoul Goff
SVP, Group Publisher: Vanessa Lopez
VP, Creative: Chrissy Kwasnik
VP, Manufacturing: Alix Nicholaeff
Publishing Director: Mike Degler
Editorial Director: Thom O'Hearn
Art Director: Stuart Smith
Senior Designer: Judy Wiatrek Trum
Editor: Alexis Sattler
Editorial Assistant: Gabrielle Cruz
Managing Editor: Shannon Ballesteros
Production Manager: Deena Hashem
Strategic Production Planner: Lina s Palma-Temena
Layout Designer: Tanya Ross-Hughes
Photographer: Ted Thomas
Prop Stylist: Elena P. Craig

REPLANTED PAPER

Insight Editions, in association with Roots of Peace, will plant two trees for each tree used in the manufacturing of this book. Roots of Peace is an internationally renowned humanitarian organization dedicated to eradicating land mines worldwide and converting war-torn lands into productive farms and wildlife habitats. Roots of Peace will plant two million fruit and nut trees in Afghanistan and provide farmers there with the skills and support necessary for sustainable land use.

Manufactured in China by Insight Editions

10 9 8 7 6 5 4 3 2 1